D1742117

Acknowledgements

I wish to thank everyone involved in making this research possible, including Professor Mike Neary, Dr Sarah Amsler, Claire and Esther, my Study Buddies, all my participants, and the late Joyce Canaan.

I will also be forever in debt to my dearest husband Alwyn, and our three sons Kevin, David, Carl, and their families who have given me so much love throughout my life and throughout this long journey, from student to teacher, thank you so much. I dedicate this book to you with my gratitude for the past, the present and my hopes for the future.

Abstract

The aim of the research was to explore the effect of teaching sociology through transformational pedagogical practices on the student learning experiences in an English FE College as well as the experience of teachers making use of transformation teaching practices. The research project was grounded in literature on the critical theory of teaching and learning (Freire 1996, hooks 1994, Allman 2010, Amsler 2014, Canaan, 2010, McLaren 2006, Neary 2012, Roggero 2011). A key feature of transformational teaching practice and the social theory that underpins it is the emphasis on the power of human agency and the ability of individuals to transform their own historical and material conditions. The qualitative research methods used reflect the power of human subjectivity and included narrative life stories and semi-structured interviews. Twenty seven participants took part in the research consisting of 15 current, and 5 former Sociology Undergraduates and 7 teachers on the programme, including myself. This work was done at the HE Institution where I work as a lecturer. The research was written in an innovative, humanised style in order to reflect the on-going and developmental praxis associated with critical and transformational teaching practices.

Contents Page

Chapter One, the

Introduction   1

Chapter Six, Conclusions 154

'Tell me about your experience of education since leaving school please'

Appendix Four

Table Four Examples of Descriptive Responses, Interview Question 2

'Tell me how teaching practices have impacted on your learning inside,

and outside of class – in a positive and negative way'.

Appendix Five

Table Five, Responses to Key Words (Prompts)Interview Question 4

'I have a list of words that describe the themes I think are important regarding student learning experiences which I would like to share and discuss with you. But before we discuss these themes would you rank them in order of what you think are the most important, please'

Appendix   Six

Table Six, Summary and Overview of Responses given to the Key words (Prompts)

Appendix Seven

My   transcript   produced   from   the   interview   questions

Chapter One

Introduction

The research explored how teaching approaches and practices which rely upon interaction and critical thought can have a profound effect upon Undergraduate students, teacher's educational experiences and their social lives. The teaching practice examined in this research is transformational teaching, including critical pedagogy traditionally associated with the work of Freire and bell hooks among others. The policy context for the research is associated with the increasing levels of a neoliberalist framework in educational institutions. The Riverside East College (the fictional name given to the Research Case, which should not be confused with any other College with a similar name) is a Further Education (FE) College in England where Higher Education (HE) provision takes place. The participants were Sociology Undergraduates and teachers working on one particular HE programme. The methodology was narrative stories and semi-structured interviews. A key aspect of the research is my own positionality and subjectivity as a participant and teacher on the programme.

The Author's writing style and Pedagogy of Hope within this thesis

As the author, and participant, within this research about critical thinking and the overwhelming importance of interaction and dialogue within the learning environment, I intend to fully commit this thesis to that teaching and learning approach. Throughout this thesis I will be communicating with you, the reader, through my own dialogue, and the research participants' responses as a form of dialogue. When writing the dialogue between you the reader and the participants, including me, the quotations will be written in italics. In addition I will be providing dialogues in the form of quotes from the literature of Freire, hooks, Neary, and Amsler amongst others in the hope that we can learn and create new knowledge together during this journey of educational exploration. The quotes used from the authors will not be written in italics in order to distinguish their words as references rather than the quotes from the participants.

As this qualitative research is very much about engaging you, the reader, with the participants, including me, atRiverside East College, like Cresswell, (2007, p.46), I consider it is very important that 'The researcher writes persuasively so that the reader experiences 'being

13

there.'… 'The writing is clear, engaging, and fullof unexpected ideas. The story and findings become believable and realistic,accurately reflecting all the complexities that exist in real life. The bestqualitative studies engage the reader.' In view of the 'many complexities' that exist throughout our human lives, this research will be written in a style that reflects the 'humanisation of the curriculum' (Freire, 1996) throughout.

This thesis can therefore be thought of as a unique learning environment where discussions and dialogues will become a process in itself towards a journey of creating new knowledge and agency. The aim is to let a different type of 'voice' speak that appeal to those who have previously been oppressed by their educational experiences. Together we will have gained a new and 'humanised' educational experience and work towards liberating ourselves from forms of teaching and learning experiences that maintain and enforce dominant neoliberal ideologies within society. This thesis will therefore be my own version and interpretation of 'Teaching to Transgress' (hooks, 1996) within a Further Education College that provides Higher Education located in a sleepy rural environment in England. A more detailed account of the HE in FE environment at the Riverside East College, and how this 'Learning Landscape' (Neary et al. (2010) has been a major factor in the research will be provided in the review of literature (Chapter Two).

Conceptualising the Problem area

The problem area addressed, and contextualised within this research, was about the current crisis within the educational system in England today (Neary, 2012, Amsler, 2014, Allman, 2010). Neary et al. propose that as all teaching is political, how, and what is taught in English Universities is being influenced more and more by the neoliberalist marketisation of education, and capitalist policies, rather than the promotion of scholarly goals involving critical thinking teaching practices. As a HE Sociology teacher I consider that this crisis in education can be challenged by raising the awareness of the situation and encouraging critical thinking within transformational teaching practices, (Freire, 1996).This method of teaching is, however, in itself problematic as it involves teaching in a style that encourages feelings of agency within Sociology Undergraduates, and their teachers. This style of teaching can be viewed as 'Teaching to Transgress' (hooks, 1994), which may engender a sense of fear and anxiety (Freire, 1996, Shor and Freire,

1987, Fromm, 1961). The challenge to overcome these fears and engender the pedagogy of hope (Amsler, 2014) and 'Crack' Capitalist influences (Holloway, 2010) specifically within HE education is, therefore, the problem that is addressed within this research.

Context of Concerns regarding the Research Problem

The problem area addressed in this research is explicitly linked to my positionality and associated with two key sociological concerns, that of class and gender inequalities within the English educational system today. Due to the location of the institution where the research takes place, regrettably there were no opportunities to include another key sociological issue regarding social inequalities, that of race, although clearly there are explicit links between class and race, and class and gender.

The Political Underpinning of the Research

Ironically perhaps, given the rural environment of the Riverside East College, Marx's teachings provide an associated and contextualised statement when referring to 'The British Agricultural Proletariat' as he states that 'Nowhere does the antagonistic character of capitalistic production and accumulation assert itself

16

more brutally than in the progress of English agriculture' (Marx,1867, Capital, Volume 1 p.473).

Later on in this research, issues surrounding the effects of how capitalist and neoliberalist policies are impacting upon the teaching practices in Universities, including the choices of topics available for study (Amsler, 2014) are discussed. The pressure upon Universities to promote Undergraduate courses as a market driven economy rather than the scholarly pursuit of knowledge is also a concern of mine and many academics (Neary, 2012, Canaan, 2010, Allman, 2010, Amsler, 2014).

Furthermore I am concerned that if students only receive a banking style of teaching they will not become aware of their own potential agency to challenge social inequalities and as such the possibility to 'Crack Capitalism' (Holloway, 2010) will be limited.

The Research Paradigm

The research paradigm or framework for the research is a Constructivist approach and methodology. The choice of a Constructivist methodology for this qualitative research is because it is my contention that the prior teaching practices the participants experienced constructed their view of reality and as such had an

17

effect upon their educational experiences and ontology. As Cresswell (2003, p.18) points out:

> 'a qualitative approach is one in which the inquirer often makes knowledge claims based primarily on constructivist perspectives (i.e., the multiple meanings of individual experiences, meanings socially and historically constructed. with an intent of developing a theory or pattern) or advocacy/participatory perspectives (i.e., political, issue-oriented, collaborative. or change oriented) or both. It also uses strategies of inquiry such as narratives, phenomenologies, ethnographies, grounded theory studies, or case studies. The researcher collects open-ended emerging data with the primary intent of developing themes from the data.'

Ontological and Epistemological Positions

With consideration to the participants ontology, and mine as the researcher, I refer to the explanation given by Cresswell, (2007, p.16) who states that 'The *ontological* issue relates to the nature of reality and its characteristics. When researchers conduct qualitative research, they are embracing theidea of multiple realities'. With regard to interpreting the participants ontological position, I consider that as I have known and worked with them at the Regional East College for several years my epistemological position mirrors the description given by Cresswell, (2005, p.18) who states that:

> 'With the *epistemological* assumption, conducting a qualitative study means that researchers try to get as close as

possible to the participants being studied. In practice, qualitative researchers conduct their studies in the 'field,' where the participants live and work -these are important contexts for understanding what the participants are saying'.

As a participant, my own educational narrative is included in the research in order to explore how my epistemology and ontology has been constructed and the influence this has had upon the research design, and my transformational style of teaching.

Ethical Considerations

All standard ethical procedures such as participant confidentiality and data protection were observed when carrying out this research. Full permission for the research to take place at the Riverside East College was given, and the University of Lincoln who are supervising the work.

Methodology

The participants' accounts of their life stories and their educational experiences were generated through narrative life stories incorporated within semi structured interviews. The participants' responses informed the research by providing links between the theoretical framework and the Review of the Literature covered in Chapter Two. The information gained from these qualitative methods was used to explore how the teaching practices the participants' had experienced affected their educational and everyday lives.

Participants

Fifteen current students on the course from all three years (five from each year) were given the opportunity to discuss how their prior teaching practices related to their present educational experiences. The five current students from each year and five previous students were selected to explore whether the time periods when they had experienced the transformational style of teaching proved to be a significant factor.

Five previous students from the course provided information relating to changes or transformations following the conclusion of their studies. Seven teachers who had successfully completed the same course were asked if their experience of being taught in a transformational style reflected upon their own teaching practices. As a participant, my responses to the semi- structured interview questions formed part of the data collection.

Sampling Procedures

The participants who met the above criteria, as teachers, current and previous students, volunteered to take part in the research as a result of a poster displayed within the teaching area of the Riverside East College. As the invitation to participate attracted more participants than needed individuals meeting the sampling criteria were selected on a first come, first served basis. As a teacher and Course Director of the Social Science Teaching Team for this Undergraduate course I was also a participant, as a key aspect of the research is my own positionality and subjectivity.

Justification for the Criteria and Sample of Participants

The reason 15 of the current students and 7 current teachers were sampled was that all of the information gained was timely and developmental and demonstrated their ongoing experience of the course. The graduate students who had completed their studies on this course were sampled as they were able to reflect upon their former progress and any transformational effects in their entirety from start to finish. These graduate students had completed the course within a varied time period ranging over 1 to 10 years.

Information gained from the current and previous students in this research focused upon the prior teaching practices from their tutors as young adults, and at undergraduate level rather than that of primary, early years. The 7 teacher participants, as members of the Social Science Teaching Team were also considered to be beneficial participants for the research as they had all been taught by me using the same teaching practices. The narrative interviews provided opportunities to explore whether the manner they were taught is reflected in their own teaching practices.

Research Questions

The Research Questions below were generated as a result of my positionality and life experiences, both as a student, a teacher, the relevant literature, and the methodology (to be discussed further in Chapter Three). The Research Questions were also developed as an effective and appropriate qualitative methodology in order to generate reliable and appropriate data.

The Research Questions were therefore;

1. What was it in particular that promoted any feelings of empowerment and agency for the Student Participants during

their classroom experiences of transformational teaching at Riverside East College?

2. Did any changes of feelings of empowerment and agency for the Student Participants affect them in their everyday lives?

3. What was it in particular that promoted feelings of empowerment and agency for the Teacher Participants, both during and following their classroom experiences of transformational teaching at Riverside East College as my students? Did the impact of their own student experiences of transformational teaching influence their current teaching practices at the Riverside East College?

The Riverside East College (The Teaching Environment/ Learning Landscape)

The institution where the research took place is mainly associated with FE courses although HE has been taught there for several years. I have taught HE Sociology at the Riverside East College since 1996 working within my role of the Course Director and lecturer. During this period I have taught all of the members of the current HE Social Science teaching team. I am therefore well known to the team members and students over this lengthy period of time.

One of the main reasons given by the Riverside East College students, who wish to study for their Degree locally, rather than in a University setting, was that they know and trust staff who taught them previously on Access or A Level courses. The familiarity of the tutors and their teaching practices was a factor as to why the students chose to study within this environment.

The transformational teaching practices the students had experienced at the Riverside East Collegewere however the main areas of focus for this research. The teacher participants who had been taught in a transformational style were given the opportunity to reflect upon how these experiences had impacted upon their own teaching practice.

The teaching practices associated with the environmental factors at Riverside East College and within this particular 'learning landscape' as associated with Neary et al. (2010) was given credence throughout the research and referred to in more depth within the review of literature.

Student and Teacher Identities/Positionality –Gender, Race, and Class at the Riverside East College

At the Teaching Environment where the research took place there were a much higher proportion of females than males studying on the Sociology Course. During the period when the research was undertaken there were approximately 60 students studying on the course, consisting of 56 females and 4 males. With regard to the teaching team, 4 were female and 3 were male. The higher proportion of females to males was also reflected in the participant sample in that 20 were female and 7 were males. Although clearly there was a higher ratio of male participants in the sampling frame than in the whole population of the course, this was due to 3 of these being teachers, in order to include each member of the teaching team.

The higher number of female students at Riverside East College reflects the National UK trends according to Ratcliffe, (2013) who raised the 'Gender Gap' in an article in the Guardian newspaper (29/01/2013). Although Ratcliffe proposed that the increase in female Undergraduates is dependent upon the type of course available for study there still appeared to be a reduction of males wishing to study at University in the UK. Ratcliffe provided data obtained over a 5 year period which clearly indicated that, for example, in the academic year 2011/2012, 64.5% of females obtained a Social Science Degree compared to 35.5% of males. The predominance of females gaining a Degree in Education was even more noticeable in that only 19.6% of males obtained this qualification, compared to 80.4% of females. As many of our students undertake a career in Education and Social Science these National Statistics do reflect the predominance of females on the Sociology course, and the participant sample at Riverside East College.

The lack of many students from a diversity of cultures studying on the course at Riverside East College was also reflected in the participant sample. The subject of race and ethnic diversity was however, discussed in great depth during the teaching on the course. Regrettably, from a humanised type of pedagogy, these discussions were somewhat limited, due to the lack of students familiar with a variety of cultures who may have been able to provide narratives of real life experiences. The very low numbers of students from different cultures studying at the Riverside East College does however reflect the research by Sims (2007) who provided statistics to show that in 60% of UK Universities the ethnic minority populations are less than 10%.

Sims (2007, p.1) proposed that the 'University is a space that greatly influences the individual's political and social consciousness and this community, though constantly changing and evolving according to its members, is an important location in building a successful multi-ethnic society.' This statement seems to suggest that by scholarly academic study, individuals can, and do gain an enhanced sense of social consciousness and as such transformational effects are achieved. Furthermore, Sims (2007, p.1) suggests that even when 'students who may not have personal interactions with others of a different race or ethnicity but are enrolled in an institution that sustains positive race relations still report higher acceptance towards others'. In this respect I consider that the teaching practices at the Riverside East College are influential in challenging oppressive power structures by raising awareness of these issues within society.

With regard to the participants' awareness and recognition of their class positions at the Riverside East College, the research by Canaan

(2011, p.28) provided enlightenment as to the 'seemingly puzzling engagement with what I call 'processes of classification'. Canaan (2011) relates that during 2005-2006, and 2008-2009 her students studying on a Social Identities module did not consider that, for them, class identification had any importance. According to Canaan (2011) there was however an increase in the students level of their personal levels of class engagement during 2009 -2010. Canaan, (2011, p.28) proposes that this increased level of engagement may have been directly associated with the 'deepening economic and political climate of polarisation separating the wealthy elite from all others was impacting student engagement with this aspect of their identities'.

The increased level of student engagement with their class identification during a period when employment prospects became increasingly competitive seems to suggest that any solidarity that working class individuals may have had was questionable and somewhat fluid. Furthermore, Canaan (2011), suggested that 'a class war' was instigated following the reduction of traditional working class industries during the Thatcher period of power, resulting in a societal attack upon working class values. As such, poverty became more of an individual's failure to budget effectively, rather than anything associated with a collective economic responsibility of government. In this respect any perceived blame upon the individual for their economic status could account for the working class students identities at the Riverside East College demonstrated by ther low levels of personal self-esteem and confidence.

As the rural geographical location of Riverside East College is situated in an area where traditional employment involves working 'on the land' this may indicate as to why some of the participants could be identified as working class when they first embark upon the sociology course. In a similar manner to Canaan's study, however, the students did not seem to fully engage with their class identities on a personal level, until they began to consider their employment prospects for the future. In this respect the participants' may have begun to identify themselves as being able to move beyond the possible limitations of working class opportunities, and as such shifted their perceived class position to that of a middle class graduate. Alternatively, as a result of the critical thinking teaching practices and experiences at the Riverside East College, they may have become more aware of, and then actively challenged their class identification and positionality as being inevitable and 'normal'.

My Identification, Positionality and the Effects upon the Research

My belief that life experiences and the researcher's positionality are the key influences upon what is researched, how it is researched and the conclusions drawn from the generated data is supported by Louis and Barton (2002,p.2) who state:

> 'Given that many roles make up our lives … we realise that we need to be aware of how our life experiences shape what type of research we choose to do, who we choose to work within our research, and how we analyse that process in the end.'

The following dialogue, regarding my positionality will provide a summary of my educational life experiences and demonstrate why I have chosen this topic for my research. The account of my positionality will also provide enlightenment as to why I believe that qualitative methods using life experiences as narratives produces such a rich and valid amount of data. My positionality as a working class female also provides justifications as to why I consider the application of life experiences are a highly appropriate method to contextualise this research within a neoliberalist educational system.

A Narrative Account, my own Classed and Gendered experiences of Education

The following narrative demonstrates how my own life has been transformed by education. As a child I was fortunate enough to gain a scholarship to attend a very expensive single sex Grammar School. Although my working class parents seemed to be pleased that I had been given this opportunity there was an expectation that this was a waste of time as I was 'only a girl – who would just get married to the boy next door' and, therefore, did not warrant any 'special' education. There were also financial problems associated with a working class girl attending an expensive Grammar School that largely consisted of boarding pupils from wealthy backgrounds. The very expensive school uniform had to be purchased from specialised up market shops and the school educational trips involved Mediterranean Cruises which obviously my parents could not afford for me to go on.

Thinking back on my experiences at school, and as an adult learning about the class system in sociology I can now reflect upon how even the way I talked did not fit in with my educators. As I was born and brought up in Bedford my accent was similar to that of a cockney Londoner which was clearly disapproved of, and as a result the school insisted I had elocution lessons to try and rid me of this. Funnily enough this did me a good turn because although my accent did not change a great deal I learned to love the poetry and Shakespeare sonnets I had to quote.

Perhaps one of the most humiliating experiences for me concerning my school education was when a list of the students whose parents had paid their dinner money for the term was posted up in the classroom. All of the other pupils had 'paid' written by their names – whereas by my name was written in large capital letters FREE. I believe these humiliating and difficult educational experiences had a profound effect upon me as a working class female child which continued to develop into adulthood. Oddly enough the prophecies of my parents became reality when I did marry at a very young age and education became something that other people did. I felt totally excluded from the educational system because it did not apply to people like me.

Following my marriage at seventeen it seemed the 'natural' and expected thing for me to become a mother – this was what working class girls did. By the time I was twenty five years old I had three children and was forced to take any low paid part-time employment that fitted in with my role of wife and mother. These jobs did not need any qualifications and were freely available as no one else wanted them as they tended to be seasonable and temporary – much like the zero contract jobs are at the moment – which as far as I can see now are a perfect example of Marx's Reserve Army of Labour. (Marx, Capital, 1867, vol. 1, p.440)

> 'If a surplus labouring population is a necessary product of accumulation or of the development of wealth on a capitalist basis, this surplus-population becomes, conversely, the lever of capitalistic accumulation, nay, a condition of existence of the capitalist mode of production. It forms a disposable industrial reserve army, that belongs to capital quite as absolutely as if the latter had bred it at its own cost'.

I first learnt of the Reserve Army of Labour notion when I started to study sociology for my first GCSE qualification as a mature student – and it resonated with me straight away as it seemed to reflect my life experiences so very much. Although at that point I did not have any sophisticated academic skills to fully understand what this was all about, I did recognise that all of the menial jobs my friends and I had done to try and earn some money to supplement our meager incomes came into this category. We had worked in jobs such as making thousands of Christmas crackers or fruit picking for an absolute pittance. Then when these commodities were not 'in season' we were no longer needed until the next year. The bosses who hired us had no problem using individuals when needed and getting rid of them when they did not. I was reminded of how similar Marx's reserve army of labour was to zero hour contracts when I read an article in the Guardian (August 4th 2013) which looked at this similarity. The article supported my viewpoint by asking: 'zero-hours contract workers- the new reserve army of labour? Karl Marx would see zero-hour contracts for what they are: rank exploitation – the type of working conditions that spawned trade unions in the first place'.

I can recognise this type of exploitation in the form of zero hour contracts now due to my sociological studies in education. I suppose this is another reason as to why I want my students to become aware and enlightened of the exploitation that goes hand in hand with capitalism. I want them to rebel against injustice and exploitation and to take action against any form of oppression and injustice that is happening now both in England and globally. I want them to gain a sense of agency as individuals and realise that just because a system such as capitalism exists today – it has not always been there, so it does not have to always be there in the future. Together we can as Holloway (2010) suggests 'Crack Capitalism' by raising levels of awareness and taking action against it.

The rebellious culture of the late sixties and seventies also had an effect upon me in that one day after an acrimonious argument with my boss I realised I could not stand his insults any longer or the increasing demands made in terms of my workload. So I just walked out of the shop where I worked and into a local FE College and signed up to study Psychology and Sociology. In fear and trepidation I started studying at 'O' Level followed by 'A' Level and then on to an Open University course. Studying for the Open University was great for me as I could still go to work and look after my husband and family. It was difficult though to fit everything in and it was quite common for me to walk to the post office box with my completed assignment at 2.30am and then get up at 7.00am to go to work – although I was able to do this as because of my very low income, the fees were free.

I then started a full time Degree course in 1989 because at that time students were given Grants to study which worked out about the same as my previous wages. Thinking back it was probably very unwise to undertake a full time Degree course and still continue with my Open University course – but I did it and ended up with two Degree's with Honours in Sociology and Psychology. I was then encouraged to do an MSc Masters in Applied Psychology as I was told by the University that I could fund the course by taking out a 'Career's Development Loan'. Ironically perhaps, as I did not have a favorable employment record of income I was refused the loan but due to a very kind lecturer arranging a fee waiver for me I was able to continue with my studies. This all happened in the early 1990's and I felt I was really fortunate to be able to gain funding for my education, especially as a working class married female with three small children and a husband to support, as unfortunately my husband has been unable to work since 1989 due to ill health. Having spoken to friends and colleagues who were in a similar position in the 1990's it seemed many such funding opportunities disappeared around that time. So they did not have the same educational chances I had and as such they were not able to continue with their HE or Postgraduate studies. So I consider I was lucky especially as when I gained the MSc qualification I was able to start a teaching career.

My love of education continued to grow – I wanted to know more and help others to learn too – especially those from a disadvantaged background like me. So I started teaching for the Open University – and because the tutors were given fee waivers I studied for an MA in Education. By this time I had five part time teaching jobs and still studying for my second Master's Degree in Education with the Open University as well as working for them too. I finally secured a full time job at the Riverside East College teaching sociology and psychology A Levels, Access and Degree programmes – that was twenty years ago.

As I progressed in my job I was asked to develop a full time Social Science Degree programme which I did – very successfully. It was then that I started to realise that my Undergraduate students were often just like me brought up to have very low educational expectations and accept they would always be affected detrimentally by their class and gender. I felt I had to do something about this – help them to see that it does not always have to be their birth right to be dominated by societal influences that ensured they had to 'know their place' and status in life. Education not only changed my life it could change theirs too – so I encouraged them to challenge the predetermined norms and values they were taught. Although I did not realise it at the time I was teaching in a transformational teaching style – and it was working, as my students continually told me they had been transformed as a result of studying on the Degree programme.

Since I started this research I have come to realise just how much life experiences can affect my students as it has done me. I also realise that I can now identify just how much the dominant ideologies of capitalism can affect working class children and determine whether they will ever have an opportunity to study and gain enough qualifications to break free from social inequalities, as individuals, and to recognize these social divisions collectively within their studies. I also know that as a teacher I have a responsibility to encourage the students to challenge these dominant ideologies – and they can do this through education if they become agents of change, with a desire to work towards a more equalitarian society. Clearly my life experiences and those of my students and teachers can be contextualised within key changes and political influences throughout history. This is why I consider my positionality and the application of the participants' life experiences are highly appropriate to contextualise this research within an increasing neoliberalist educational system.

In this sense I consider that this research will truly reflect the work of Freire in that within the Foreword of Freire, (1996, p.13) Shaull states:

> 'I find a dialogue with the thought of Paulo Freire an exciting venture. Fed up as I am with the abstractness and sterility of so much intellectual work in academic circles today, I am excited by a process of reflection which is set in a thoroughly historical context, which is carried on in the midst of a

struggle to create a new social order and thus represents a new unity of theory and praxis'.

As I consider that Universities and educational experiences are very much in 'the midst of a struggle' *concerned with the increasing influences of neoliberalism, this research involving teachers who are currently teaching in a transformational and political style, and the effects of these practices upon Undergraduates, is the antipathy of* 'abstractness and sterility'. *The 'struggle' and challenges of teaching in a humanised style that can induce a sense of fear within employment situations and personal levels of confidence are discussed within Chapter 5 (Thematic Data Analysis) and Chapter Six (Conclusions). I also think that within this research as I will be entering into a dialogue with participants, authors, including of course Paulo Freire, and by reviewing his thoughts and work, which for me, like Shaull is also* 'an exciting venture'.

In Chapter Two (the Review of Literature) the manner in which my positionality has influenced the research design is expanded upon in more depth within a comprehensive Review of the Literature. Within this chapter I focus upon Freire, (1996) hooks, (1994) Holloway, (2010) Amsler, (2011) Canaan, (2011) Allman, (2010) McLaren, (2006) and Neary, (2012) as key practitioners of

41

transformational and critical pedagogy teaching practices, and associated with particular interpretations and viewpoints regarding this form of educational practice. The inclusion of a review of this Literature underpins the research and provides the main theoretical framework.

In Chapter Three (Methodology) the design of the research was developed and justified with regard to the conceptual framework, my ontology, and epistemology. The methods used to obtain the data; narrative life stories and semi structured interviews, were described and reported upon. Within this chapter the participant selection and sampling process was also demonstrated, followed by an explanation as to why the pilot interviews instigated changes and amendments to the data collection procedures. An explanation as to the development of the consolidated interview procedures, including ethical considerations was then provided. The latter part of Chapter Three provided an overview of the data coding and thematic analysis of each interview question associated with the developmental stages of pedagogy (Freire, 1996), and Sweet (1998). Finally in Chapter Three a description of how transformational teaching in the classroom at

Riverside East College is linked and applied to the key processes raised within the Review of Literature.

Within Chapter Four (Research Findings) an overall summary of the key findings is produced. Each of the six interview questions, including the alternative question for the teachers, coded as 6TP, was reported upon. A summary of the findings and participant responses is provided at the conclusion of each interview question review. The additional research findings regarding the use of metaphors by the participants during the interviews were then reported upon. Finally, an initial review of the research findings directs the reader to the production of the thematic data analysis to be covered in the next chapter.

In Chapter Five (Thematic Data Analysis) the thematic research data was consolidated with the interview questions and the review of literature. The key thematic findings that arose from the data were summarised and supported by examples of the participant responses. The justification and review of the methodology was also reported upon in this chapter in order to assess the consistency and trustworthiness of the findings, including the metaphor analysis. Finally at the end of Chapter Five a summary of the thematic analysis of the findings leads directly into the last chapter and the conclusions drawn from this research.

The final Chapter Six (Conclusions) provides a reflective and reflexive summary of the whole research, and takes the reader through the key salient issues raised and addressed throughout. Each of the key conclusions was illustrated with one or two quotes from the participants, including me. In this manner an explicit or implicit voice is given to everyone involved in the research, including the authors referred to in the review of literature. The research quest to address how teaching practices can have a transformational influence upon learners, and challenge the current pedagogy of fear through an enhanced sense of agency, is given consideration in light of a pedagogy of hope for the future.

Chapter Two, the Review of Literature

Introduction

The Process and Development of the Review of Literature

When I first embarked on writing this review of literature I gave some serious thought as to what a review of literature actually is – and why is it an important element of the research itself. After reading a great deal of literature on this subject I have come to the conclusion that it is a form of research in itself. Furthermore, although this may seem something of an obvious statement this form of research is dependent upon the researcher's own active role as the author. As pointed out by Murray (2002, p.101) 'it is the thesis writers' version of the literature, their selection and arrangement of their summaries and critiques'. As the topic of this thesis was about exploring how educational experiences and teaching practices can have a transformational effect upon learners, and teachers, it seemed apt to look at how, as the author, I approached this review of literature.

I began the review of literature by asking myself who I was writing this for. Again the answer to this question seemed quite simple in that although I wrote this review of literature to learn what previous authors have written about the topic, I also wanted to find out how they came to their own conclusions and thinking processes. I also needed to think about where my ideas have come from about the topic and what methods should I use to find out. After thinking this through I came to the conclusion that the review of literature was a transformative experience in itself for me.

My initial problem with regard to writing the review of literature was not the lack of texts and journal articles about the topic; in fact it was quite the reverse. There has been a great deal of theoretical writing on the subject of transformational teaching practices especially with regard to critical thinking and how this can affect students becoming potential agents of change. My first problem was, therefore, what to include and what to omit from the review, although this is clearly not a unique situation for my research, and something that I am sure all researchers experience. By contrast, I initially thought there was a paucity of literature with regard to the specific practical application of critical thinking teaching practices concerning Undergraduates studying HE courses in FE Colleges in England. I came to this conclusion at first, but that was before my levels of conscientization developed more and I started to discover that critical thinking and transformation practices were legion, and not just in education.

Murray (2002, p.106) looks at the relationships between students gaining knowledge from reading previous literature and writing their own review of literature, and stated 'One of the issues that arises from working with students on literature reviews is the complex relationship between thinking, knowledge production, and the writing process'. As my subjective interpretation and the manner in which I selected and wrote about the literature covered in this chapter was a key element throughout this research, I considered that the development of my own writing style was also an important factor.

In order to take ownership of this review of literature, therefore, it was written within the remit of my own writing skills and the ability to conduct this research. I took the responsibility and the risk of researching and writing up this review of literature in a style that for me made sense in terms of my own experiences of 'conscientization', and the banking style of teaching (Freire, 1996) rather than stick rigidly to the academic conventional writing style so often insisted upon in traditional English Universities. In this respect

I amalgamated the literature covered in this review with the 'real world' educational experiences of the participants, including my own experiences. The reason for including the participants' illustrations of real world experiences was to follow Freire's lead regarding the need to humanise my research by integrating these experiences with theory as part of the educational process. By integrating examples of real life, previous educational experiences, such as school, which may be thought of as 'deposits' I wanted to avoid using the banking system myself, by demonstrating that this review of literature was written as a *process* and not a product. As the researcher, and as a student, I am continually reviewing how previous research affects my own version of reality, and as such I too have experienced a form of transformation during this process. I continued to explore my own transformational processes, and that of the participants, within the presentation of the findings and the concluding chapters.

I demonstrated this somewhat innovative style of writing, by using the terminology of a teaching 'approach' and a teaching 'practice' interchangeably. Furthermore as the literature generated the Research Questions and the methodology, and ultimately the interpretation of the findings, I broke free from academic dictates and 'humanised' my writing style to accommodate for what I considered to be appropriate and contextualised within this process.

The Teaching Environment and the Learning Landscape

An important aspect of this work is the teaching and learning environment. This is particularly important in terms of gender, race and class, although this is not usually considered in the literature on learning landscapes in education.

With regard to gender Neary et al. (2010, p.44) consider that "Women writers have made a significant contribution to debates about academic space" with regard to the work of Virginia Woolf (2008) concerning the denial of women to intellectual reading spaces at an Oxbridge College. Although within contemporary Universities and Colleges in the UK this would probably be considered illegal, discriminatory and morally wrong, Neary et al. (2010) report that these issues have still not been fully addressed or resolved. The difference between a 'Private Space' and a Public space is according to Neary et al., (2010, p.44) described as being a gender issue. The Private space can be thought of somewhere women feel their "sense of belonging…emotionality, sensual delight, physical pleasure and affection for particular locations…Public space, on the other hand, is dominated by men and represents sites of fear, unease and insecurity for women".

Within the Riverside East College I think this is not such a frightening 'public space' for women as they do express feeling a 'sense of belonging' here, in that they are not only familiar with the learning space and environment itself, but with the teachers as well. This could explain why there are many more female students than males studying on this particular course, and as to why, they feel they have an opportunity to gain a voice, and the associated enhanced feelings of self-confidence within their teaching sessions. The issue surrounding the effects upon teacher and student relationships, and the sense of a 'community of learners,' is addressed later on within this chapter.

Neary et al. (2010, p.47) also propose that the voice of the academic can be enhanced by involving them into the debate as to what the purpose of higher education actually is, when learning spaces are developed.

'The academic voice can be further enhanced by challenging academics to intellectualise the debate about teaching and learning space by reference to the custom and tradition, principles and preoccupations of their own subject area.'

Traditional learning spaces described by Woolf (2008, p.199) as being built with "carved stone and stained glass" should be replaced by cheaper experimental learning spaces to reflect youth, poverty and learning resources that are new and constantly changing. Woolf (2008, p.199) clearly proposes that before designing new learning spaces for women in particular, consideration should be given to "what is the aim of education, what kind of a society, what kind of human being it should seek to produce". The environmental learning space at the Riverside East College reflects Woolf's proposal in that the teaching rooms equipped with tables and chairs provides opportunities for small group discussions and teaching with the aim of a critical, questioning style.

Within the Riverside East College the values of the institution are also clearly met with the provision of a designated HE teaching area, and there is also a 'flexi-space' that can be used as a Conference Centre when required. In addition, the HE teaching takes place over two Semesters with the provision of two twelve week blocks whereas the FE teaching is conducted over three terms providing thirty six weeks of teaching. The differences in HE and FE teaching weeks can be accommodated for within this type of Learning Landscape with the provision of a 'just in time' teaching availability for short periods. In particular the HE teaching rooms can be used for short FE vocational courses or additional FE examination revision spaces etc. In this manner the needs of both HE and FE can be successfully integrated within the same learning environment.

With regard to class it could however be argued that regardless as to how well an FE institution accommodates for the teaching of HE some individuals may feel pressurised to study at one of the highest ranked UK Universities in the hope of securing greater academic status for future employment prospects within an increasingly commercialised capitalist framework. In this respect therefore the decision to study at a HE institution rather than within a predominantly FE Institution may not be a result of an individual choice, but rather the wider structures and pressures of class issues within society.

HESA the Higher Education Statistics Agency provides a league table ranking of the English Universities in addition to a vast amount of data concerning these institutions. HESA (2014) ranked the

University of Cambridge as the highest (number one), followed by the University of Oxford (number two) and the London School of Economics as number three. This information is freely available for potential students and parents which may influence the choice of an English University for HE study. There is however very little or no interest in even considering Universities for some HE students actively studying in FE institutions according to the Institute of Education (IOL 2014). According to an extensive study by the IOL (2014) there is a significant number of HE students studying in FE institutions (one in twelve) for a variety of reasons such as financial, familiarity of teaching staff and location.

The research findings identified by the IOL (2014) are also clearly supported within the Riverside East College. The vast majority of the Riverside East College HE students can generally be thought of as non- traditional students in that they are mainly mature females with children living in a socially economically deprived area. In this respect there are financial and geographically accessible advantages for my students to study locally rather than at a University, although regretfully there have still been occasions when these students have been unable to attend lectures due to financial reasons such as travel or child care costs.

In the Riverside East College there is also recognition of a need for students to purchase more academic resources due to the limitations of those within the FE institution compared to those in a University which has resulted in a reduction of fees. Other financial reasons given for a reduction of fees for the majority of HE in FE students are identified by the IOL (2014) as 'The cost of providing HE courses in colleges is believed by college managers to be lower than HEIs- mainly a consequence of lower average teaching costs, greater staff productivity, more limited expenditure on learning infrastructure and fewer social facilities'.

Overwhelmingly however the main reason I have been given by my current and previous students as to why they wish to study for their Degree at the Riverside East College is that they know and trust the staff who have taught them previously on Access or A Level courses which also supports the IOL (2014) research conclusions 'FE Colleges provide continuity for students who have already taken further education- level courses and offer a more supportive learning environment'. As all of the Social Science Teaching Team with the exception of myself, has taught the HE students in the Riverside East College at either Access or A Level courses they are well known and familiar within this local learning environment. The extent that the prior knowledge and relationship between teachers and students has upon their educational experiences is explored later on in this chapter and throughout this research.

Political effects upon the Learning Environment

As to whether educational experiences should be viewed as a product or a scholarly activity which engages students in critical thinking is of course one of the main questions to be addressed within my research and that of the authors within this review of literature. Robertson (2007) clearly considers that education has now become explicitly and intrinsically linked to economic factors within a neoliberalist context. Robertson, S., (2007, p.02) states:

> 'This tectonic shift has transformed how we talk about education, teachers and learners,… groups and professional associations… it has altered the conditions for knowledge production, along with the spaces and sites for claims-making around education. With education yoked more closely to national and regional economies, schools and Universities are now universally mandated to (efficiently and effectively) create the new breed of entrepreneurs and innovators; the value-driven minds who will spearhead the battle for global markets and consumers, and a bigger share of the spoils'.

55

Robertson (2007) clearly considers that there has been a shift away from an academic and scholarly focus in education towards that of a 'production of knowledge' with a neoliberalist emphasis, as also proposed by Amsler (2011, 2013), Neary (2011) Neary et al. (2012).Amsler (2010, p.21) gives credence to what seems to be happening in English HE institutions with regard to an increased emphasis on economic factors dictating what is taught, and how, by stating that:

> 'What is new, in England and other neoliberal societies, is the rapidity with which long histories of critical education are being erased from public memory- even amongst educators themselves- and the ease with which principles of critical pedagogy are reconstructed as threats to social and economic progress'.

Amsler (2010) also proposes that the neoliberalist influence in Universities has an effect upon whether or not academics are funded for research activities, which I consider is a fundamental element to critical education. Amsler (2010, p.21) provides powerful and concerning arguments by proposing that in order to gain funding for research 'performance targets' and 'benchmarking' evidence has to be achieved. Furthermore Universities in England can individually discipline researchers who do not achieve the targets set. Amsler's

(2010, p.21) concerns clearly reflect those of Freire and Shor (1986) with regard to the risk that academics take when undertaking experimental research and critical pedagogy by stating:

> 'critical debate about issues of common concern to members of a University is frowned upon as disruptive and repressed through layers of bureaucracy or the erosion of space and time for informal dialogue: where experimental mistakes in teaching are punished as incompetence - in such conditions, the forces mitigating against critical pedagogy can seem indomitable'

The Production and Marketisation of Knowledge

Neary et al. (2012, p.1) question the purpose of Universities within a neoliberalist educational environment. In light of increases in economical factors, such as University student fees, and the need to consider the production of knowledge as a commodity, the question arises as to whether working class or mature adults with limited expectations of employment opportunities will be able to become scholars in the true sense of the word. As such it would be reasonable to support the claim that Universities are in a state of crisis, torn between the need to be economical commodity and an environment that provides a platform for critical thinking, challenging a capitalist production of knowledge. Neary et al. (2012, p.1) proposes that 'Higher education as a public good – this challenges the marketisation and commodification of higher education and asks how far is it possible to promote equality through higher education by using extended and open access, student choice and the scholarship of teaching and learning.'

Neary (2012) has been a leading advocate of the concept and practice of Student as Producer, a form of transformational teaching practice grounded within the principles of 20th century avant-garde Marxism. The University of Lincoln has been heavily associated with the development of a Student as Producer project advocating the collaboration between students and academics in order to produce new knowledge. The main aim of this collaboration is that students become aware of their ability to become active subjects capable of instigating change, recognising and designing their own place within the world. In order to fulfill this aim the Student as Producer framework within the University of Lincoln gives a total commitment and great emphasis to the engagement between research and teaching. There is also an additional acknowledgement that the human attributes of creativity and desire within this framework reflect the academic values and purpose of the original and historical development of Universities.

Neary (2012) provides robust arguments to maintain that the original values of Universities have been diminished with the continual and powerful development of capitalism within contemporary society. In order to redress this imbalance the University of Lincoln has a committed policy to support academic research and engagement with the teaching of research for Undergraduates studying across all academic disciplines. At the heart of this development and policy is the recognition that in order to create and produce new knowledge the collaboration between learners and teachers needs to be strongly supported. The Undergraduate curriculum at the University of Lincoln is therefore dependent upon student research and research teaching. The collaboration between students and academics ensures that the design of the Undergraduate curriculum programme and their learning environments have developed from this joint cooperation.

Amsler's work (2011, 2013) was considered to be of primary importance to the theoretical framework and empirical research with specific regard to the need to increase levels of awareness of the marketisation of education in England and globally. At the Riverside East College the students are encouraged to learn of, and challenge the manner in which neoliberalism influences have affected what and how they are able to study at Undergraduate level. The urgent need to become aware of the historical, current and future effects of neoliberalism on the students and teachers educational experiences has become of salient importance in the theoretical and conceptional framework of this study. Amsler (2011) writing from a feminist and neo-Marxist perspective, also grounds her work in the concept and consequences of neoliberalist practices. Amsler (2011) proposes that the effects of neoliberalist practices within the U.K have affected the choice of disciplines available within Universities. Disciplines requiring critical thought have had funding cut or reduced in order to invest more economic resources into those in tune with capitalist requirements such as Business Studies. Amsler's work is particularly relevant to my research concerning the teaching practice of sociology that requires critical thought and is taught in a manner that raises awareness of capitalist issues dominating educational provision.

Amsler's research and published work is, therefore clearly concerned with the prospect of capitalist ideals as determining both academic and pedagogical issues within English Universities, which inevitably results in the oppression of critical thought within the classroom. It would seem for Amsler that unless alternative pedagogical strategies can be employed the dominant capitalist and neoliberal power structures will remain unchallenged resulting in the acceptance and maintenance of inequalities within society. The feminist and race inequalities that both Amsler and hooks (1994) raise within teaching and educational experiences will, therefore, remain unchallenged, unless individuals become aware of their own capabilities to become activists and encourage critical thought regarding power inequalities within society.

In the same manner that Freire (1996) proposes that education should be 'humanising' Amsler (2010, p.3)states that 'Perhaps we can finally accept that there are no ears to even receive arguments about the importance of humanising education, the power of ideas and research to transform the world, or the possibility of critical thought in a frighteningly possibility-limiting social system'. Within my research, therefore, I am looking at whether my students have become aware of their own agency and the ability to challenge and transform the world as subjects rather than objects by the educational and teaching practices they have experienced.

The Production and the Control of Knowledge

Gigi Roggero (2011) links what he calls 'cognitive capitalism' to a crisis in Universities by proposing that the production of knowledge is explicitly linked to the changing nature of the workforce, globally. Roggero (2011, p.03) states that 'knowledge in itself is neither good nor bad- it is a battlefield and one that is becoming central to class struggle.' In this respect Roggero suggests that there is a complex relationship between the manner in which knowledge is produced and militant class struggles. Roggero (2011, p.05) quotes Mario Tronti (1966, p.14) who proposes that 'Knowledge comes from struggle. Only he who really hates really knows.'

Furthermore Roggero (2011, p.05) adds 'as postcolonial theorists have suggested for a long time now, there is no production of knowledge that is not situated knowledge'. Roggero (2011, p.01) succinctly provides a quote from Sterling (1998) to sum up his view that education can only be thought of within a political context 'Knowledge is only knowledge. But the control of knowledge – that is politics.' Roggero makes it quite clear therefore that it is not possible to understand any transformations that take place within Universities, without giving consideration to the changes that are happening concerning production and labour. Roggero (2011, p.3) also talks of a 'double crisis' which is happening, 'the global economic crisis and the crisis of the University and the intimate relation that binds them'.

Roggero (2011) also makes it quite clear that in order to understand how knowledge can become a part of capitalist production and accumulation in terms of cognitive labour it is necessary to understand how these forces can be perpetuated. Roggero suggests that although manual labour is not disappearing, the class composition can only be changed by an increased awareness of becoming cognitive and aware of capitalist forces of knowledge production. Furthermore, students in post secondary education become cognitive producers according to Roggero (2011, p.26) who proposes that:

> 'Since the student no longer answers to the definition of labor power in formation, but becomes for all intents and purposes a cognitive producer. The University is a privileged space through which to observe the transformations... The modern

University, which found its relationship with the state the definition of its public being no longer exists'

Oppressive Power Structures, Class and Gender issues

Within this research I looked at how the participants associated oppressive power structures within their own lives and general society. In a similar fashion, to Jenkins, Filippakou, Canaan, and Strudwick, (2011), I looked at the way in which my students reflected upon whether their lives had been dictated and shaped by capitalist and oppressive practices within society. I considered that initially the students were not necessarily aware of the extent they had been oppressed by power structures within society, with particular reference to class and gender issues. Having experienced critical teaching at the Riverside East College, however, the extent to which they had become more enlightened and aware of the extent of their oppression within society was one of the main focus areas of the research. Working as transformational teachers, Jenkins et al. (2011) considered that 'As Freire (2006) and others … have long suggested, critical pedagogy underpins teaching and learning practices that seek to engender an appreciation of injustices faced in social, economic and institutional life' (Jenkins et al. 2011, p. 7).

Whether, the participants explicitly referred to issues of class and gender within their narratives was also explored. Surprisingly perhaps, the authors, Jenkins et al. (2011), found that their students failed to recognise the sociological concepts and analysis of class, in relation to their own personal lives. I considered that the use of narratives within my research would give insights into whether this was the case for the participants. The use of narratives was used to produce insights into the relationship between the teaching practices of sociology at the Riverside East College, and the identification of class and gender issues within their own personal lives and society.

The question as to what constitutes a particular class is in itself somewhat ambiguous, in that individuals may consider they are, either working class, or middle class, according to their profession, although this may be a constantly changing and fluid situation. Furthermore, individuals may relate their class to their income rather than their profession, or their traditionally held beliefs, as demonstrated within their narratives. It was necessary, therefore, to give consideration as to why individuals may think of themselves as either working class or middle class, and furthermore whether these concepts were still relevant within contemporary society.

Stuart (2012) points out that although stratifications of class can be measured by using complex measures, many people no longer identify with these classifications. Furthermore Stuart, (2012, p.26) clearly supports Archer, (2003, p.16) 'with the impact of globalisation individuals have had to take sole responsibilities for their actions…Individuals are more likely to blame themselves for life inequalities. Although as a HE lecturer I could fall under the umbrella of a 'middle class' status, my own perception of my identity is that I am most definitely working class, and always will be, to think of myself as anything other would be unthinkable, and would be a betrayal of my roots, values and upbringing. My feelings in this respect do perhaps reflect how ambiguous the issue of class identification is, and begs the question as to why individuals may attempt to define themselves in terms of class, and as to whether this is a significant factor of their identity and their versions of reality.

Critical Thinking, a Means of Escape from Oppression

As my research is specifically concerned with teaching practices associated with social inequalities, Freire (1996) was an obvious choice for my literature research especially in terms of his epic and renowned work 'The Pedagogy of the Oppressed'.Freire was born

1921 in Brazil and worked as an educator living amongst extremely poor and illiterate peasants and, therefore, had a firsthand knowledge of their lived experiences. The poverty that the peasants experienced was a key factor in terms of his educational needs in that he is cited within Gadotti (1994, p.05) as stating 'I didn't understand anything because of my hunger. I wasn't dumb. It wasn't lack of interest. My social condition didn't allow me to have an education. Experience showed me once again the relationship between social class and knowledge'.

Although clearly as my research is being conducted in an English Further Education College and my students could certainly not be regarded as suffering the same types of oppression as the Brazilian illiterate peasants Freire wrote about, theoretically and ironically there are a great deal of similarities between those educationalists and learners in Brazil. My students are almost all working class females who have usually been oppressed by their previous educational and social conditions from which they want to break free.

Freire, (1996, p.62) states 'Education as the practice of freedom - as opposed to education as the practice of domination - denies that man is abstract, isolated, independent, and unattached to the world; it also denies that the world exists as a reality apart from people'. In this respect the 'humanisation' of knowledge is clearly referred to, and acknowledged by Freire and hooks, in that individual's engage with the world in a meaningful and real manner within their everyday lives, and given the opportunity critical pedagogy and education. In addition, hooks, (1994) points out that the practice of freedom has an influence upon teachers, which she refers to as an 'engaged pedagogy' which empowers students. According to hooks, (1994, p.15), an engaged pedagogy can be:

> 'more demanding than conventional critical or feminist pedagogy. For, unlike these two teaching practices, it emphasises well-being. That means that teachers must be actively involved and committed to a process of self-actualisation that promotes their own well-being if they are to teach in a manner that empowers students.'

In this respect, I consider that teaching in a critical style that promotes empowerment for the students has also had an effect upon the Teaching Team. These feelings of transformational changes, empowerment and agency are addressed throughout the Research Questions and methodology. An engaged pedagogy can therefore be associated with this research, in that I am looking at how the teaching practices at the Riverside East College engaged with the students, the teachers, both within and outside of the classroom, or as Freire suggests interacting with the 'world' in an objective and subjective manner.

Freire (1996, p.32) suggests that 'one cannot conceive of objectivity without subjectivity,' furthermore Freire considers:

> 'To deny the importance of subjectivity in the process of transforming the world and history is naïve and simplistic. It is to admit the impossible: a world without people. The objective position is as ingenuous as that of subjectivism, which postulates people without a world. World and human beings do not exist apart from each other, they exist in constant interaction'.

The need for constant interactions between the 'World' and human beings is supported by Wright (1989, p.118) who states that 'it was Paulo Freire who suggested a way forward ... A radical theory of learning needs a theory of knowledge which avoids two extremes: one is knowledge seen as a 'thing' which must somehow be pumped into passive learners: the other, knowledge is seen as a purely individual creation ...What makes human society is a set of shared understandings and shared meanings.' At the Riverside East College it has become clear that during class discussions and small group work with both tutors and students, a shared level of understanding and meanings has been achieved, and as such the application to theory engendered a sense of multiple realties.

The Question of 'Reality' and Dominating Ideologies

The Research Questions were directly linked to the work of Freire regarding the manner in which individuals attempt to escape oppressive forces by firstly reaching a state of awareness or 'conscientization' of their plight. Conscientization is described by McLaren, (1996, p.127) as 'a deep or critical reading of common sense reality'. The manner in which this state of awareness can be achieved is by becoming actively engaged in the struggle to escape oppression and work towards a state of transformation for individuals and society as a whole. By refusing to accept that there is no escape from oppression both learners and leaders can become transformed as individuals, and consider the possibility of transforming whole societies. Freire, (1996, p.62) states 'Education as the practice of freedom - as opposed to education as the practice of domination - denies that man is abstract, isolated, independent, and unattached to the world; it also denies that the world exists as a reality apart from people'. Within teaching sessions and discussions

70

at the Riverside East College, the participants provided examples of their own 'real world' educational experiences to demonstrate how they thought they had been either oppressed or alternatively gained a sense of being liberated by them. The manner in which the teachers instigated the students to provide their own examples of real-life examples, and shared meanings of reality, was done by encouraging them to have the confidence and trust within their groups to voice their own experiences. The way in which the teachers provided opportunities for the students to gain a voice is explained in more depth at the end of Chapter Three (How we do it at Riverside East College) and within Chapter Six (Conclusions)

Within this research the key words such as oppression, freedom and democracyemerging from this review of literature are incorporated into the semi structured interviews. The key words were included in the interview questions to see whether the participants considered they had become more aware of dominant ideologies and power structures as a result of a critical approach and teaching practices.

Teaching practices, the Banking Concept of Education, and the Effects upon Students

This research was therefore initially concerned with the perceived prior teaching practices the participants had experienced, and as to, if, why, and how, the students had been taught to accept their position within society, without question. Freire (1996, p.53) referred to as the 'banking concept of education, in which the scope of action allowed to the students extends only as far as receiving, filing, and storing the deposits'. In this manner Freire proposes that the teachers literally deposit their version of reality and knowledge on to the students without any dialogue or opportunity to question this historically determined conclusion as to what are 'facts'. As a child brought up in a working class environment I can certainly relate to what Freire is referring to as a banking concept of education, having to memorise facts in a rote type fashion, there was certainly no opportunities to discuss or challenge what the teacher told you was 'real and true'. Freire, (1996, p.56) proposed that eventually however, even 'passive students and teachers who teach in the banking style will discover that:

> '[those] who use the banking approach…fail to perceive that the deposits themselves contain contradictions about reality. But, sooner or later, these contradictions may lead formerly passive students to turn against their domestication and the attempt to domesticate reality … They may perceive

through their relations with reality that reality is really a *process,* undergoing constant transformation.'

As my students repeatedly spoke of being taught in a style at school that did not provide opportunities to enter into any meaningful dialogue with their teachers, to discuss, or critically think about the topics they were being taught, this supported Freire's thought, that, 'Education thus becomes an act of depositing, in which the students are depositories and the teacher the depositor. Instead of communicating, the teacher issues communiqués and makes deposits which the students partially receive, memorize and repeat'(Freire, 1996, p.53).

Teaching Practices, the Banking Concept of Education, and the Effects upon Teachers

Within my previous role of management at the Riverside East College I was responsible for supporting the A Level teachers across the county, by providing teaching support and mentoring, and arranging regular meetings and conferences with examiners. During these meetings it became quite clear that the majority of these teachers had rigid views as to what was factually correct and acceptable within their teaching disciplines. I was saddened by the lack of critical thinking that was demonstrated within these meetings, although not totally surprised as they literally had to teach their students to write out their 'banked deposits of knowledge' (Freire, 1996) in order to pass their A Levels.

I was even more saddened when I met these A Level students as year one Undergraduate students who had applied to study at the Riverside East College with me, as I could easily recognise which of the teachers had taught them. In year one these students literally repeated the same deposits and versions of reality their teachers had demonstrated at the Management meetings. Regretfully this demonstration of the banking teaching methods and effects upon students reminded me of my late mothers narrative when she told me that children were disciplined if their writing style differed to what the teacher told them was correct, not just in content, but in the actual production of individual letters. In this manner all adults could be identified as attending a particular school as children, and being taught by a specific teacher, within a specific era and context. In this respect the teacher gave little or no credence to the context of what was taught in terms of the student's life experiences or personal interest. This effect upon students is supported by Freire (1996, p.52) who considered that within the banking system:

> 'The teacher talks about reality as if were motionless, static, compartmentalised, and predictable. Or else he expounds on a topic completely alien to the existential experience of the students. His task is to 'fill' the students with the contents of his narration- contents which are detached from reality, disconnected from the totality that engendered them and could give them significance. Words are emptied of their concreteness and become a hollow, alienated, and alienating verbosity.'

Critical and Transformational Theory

The question as to what critical theory involves is addressed within the conference paper by Amsler, Canaan, Cowden, Motta and Singh (2010), who ask whether there a difference between critical thinking and actually practicing the thought process within teaching practices? In other words could my problem of deciding what theoretical information to include and what to omit in this review of literature be divorced from the issue of practical application – or are they both one and the same? I considered that this latter question raised a lot more questions than answers, which in my opinion as an academic and proponent of critical thinking was highly laudable and an essential element of the research and critical educational experience.

In the same manner I questioned whether to use the terminology of a critical teaching 'approach' or a critical teaching 'practice'? My interpretation of a teaching approach implied thought processes and theoretical issues, whereas a 'practice' I interpreted as the actual application of theory and knowledge. The issues arising from the group of co-authors (Amsler et al. 2010, p.13) included a reference to this ambiguity by asking 'What do we mean by 'practice'? For example, need there be a division between 'theory and 'practice', or is formal academic thinking a form of political practice? In what ways can political practices be considered processes of learning and teaching?' The differentiation of theory and practice was therefore raised and clarified effectively by the guidance provided within this article.

The terminology of what constitutes critical theory can in itself be challenged, and open to critique and question. Giroux (1983) provides two types of meanings to the terminology 'critical theory'. Giroux (1983) points out that there is no universal or conclusively shared agreement as to what critical theory is, he also considers that one meaning is loosely derived from the theoretical concepts of the

76

Frankfurt School. Giroux (1983) suggests that members of the Frankfurt School attempted to rethink the meaning of critical theory in terms of the human experience rather than solely concentrating on the theoretical aspects of orthodox Marxism. Giroux, (1983) clarifies this 'rethinking' process in which human experiences could be explicitly associated with theoretical orthodox Marxist doctrines. Giroux (1983, p.27) considered that 'there was an attempt on the part of all members of the Frankfurt School to rethink and radically reconstruct the meaning of human emancipation, a project that differed considerably from the theoretical baggage of orthodox Marxism'. Within this research the notion of the human experience of emancipation is of great importance, and as such imbedded within the theoretical framework of Marxism, rather than as a polarised debate between lived experiences and theoretical concepts.

The attempts made in this research to embed critical thinking and practical lived experiences within a Marxist framework can be thought of similar to the aims of the Frankfurt School; although within this research there is a unique and innovative focus upon HE educational experiences within an FE environment. In general the research is supported by Giroux's aims (1983, p.27) with regard to theory, in that he states 'I argue…for the importance of original critical theory and the insights it provides for developing a critical foundation for a theory of radical pedagogy'.

The difference between Giroux's theoretical aims and this research is that I provide a practical demonstration as to how critical theory can be applied to HE teaching practices within an FE environment at the Riverside East College. The second aspect of critical theory, (Giroux (2001, p.05) refers to is associated with a 'self-conscious critique' and the need to:

> 'Develop a discourse of social transformation and emancipation that does not cling dogmatically to its own doctrinal assumptions. (In other words critical theory refers to both a 'school of thought' and a process of critique)…a body of work that both demonstrates and simultaneously calls for the necessity of ongoing critique, one in which the claims of any theory must be confronted with the distinction between the world it examines and portrays, and the world as it actually exists'.

These claims by Giroux (2001) are supported within this research in that it provides an ongoing self-conscious critique of theory within the 'real world' of the participants. The participants in this research demonstrate their lived experience of the 'real world' through the narrative interviews and accounts of their educational experiences in order to critique the theoretical aspects and processes of critical theory.

Allman, (2010) suggests that there is some ambiguity as to what the term critical pedagogy or as she prefers 'critical education' actually refers to. 'In the United Kingdom, as well as other countries, the term critical education is often used synonymously with radical education and education for socialism or social transformation' (2010, p.149). Allman (2010) considers that unless individuals experience education in a manner that encourages critical thought the forces of contemporary capitalism will ensure that millions of people will not achieve a sense of critical awareness and consciousness. It is therefore a matter of urgency that individuals experience critical education and not capitulate to capitalist ideology in order to avoid the 'continuing dehumanisation of millions of human beings' (Allman, 2010, p.150).

Allman also states that education should be revolutionary in order to transform society and ensure the development of a 'communist social formation advocated by Karl Marx. The need for critical education has never been greater' (Allman, 2010, p.150). The need for critical education is fundamental to Allman's proposals, as the alternative would be to train individual's to accept the detrimental consequences upon oppressed victims of capitalism as being inevitable and unavoidable. Allman does however state quite clearly that the transformation of society cannot be totally reliant upon critical education, there is also a need for men and women to develop their levels of awareness of the dangers of capitalism as associated with Marxist social theory. Allman, (2010, p.151) states:

> 'When I explain Marx's theory of consciousness, I think you will be able to discern certain parallels between his theory and a great deal of the thinking that informs educational psychology and educational theory… Marx's theory provides a much more effective theoretical basis for fostering the development of critical thinking and especially as one might expect, the development of critical dialectical conceptualisation'.

McLaren (2006, p.14) emphasises the need for underpinning educational practices with relevant theoretical concepts by stating that 'Such theoretical infrastructure is absolutely necessary for the construction of concrete pedagogical spaces in schools and in other sites where people struggle for educational change and social and political transformation'. The notion that individuals can become active agents in society and be able to change levels of inequality in terms of race and sexism clearly mirrors the ideology of hooks (1994), and in terms of oppression Freire (1996). In the same manner, Allman, (2010), McLaren, (2006) clearly gives emphasis to the political aspects of critical thinking and teaching practices. McLaren (2006, p.13) also holds the same views as Allman in that there is an urgent need to challenge the effects of neo-liberalism within education.

> 'revolutionary critical pedagogy … It draws attention to the key concepts of imperialism (both economic and military) and neo-liberalism and, by tacking around the work of Karl Marx, Paulo Freire, and Antonio Gramsci … it brings some desperately needed theoretical ballast to the teetering critical educational tradition.'

Amsler (2013) describes her approach to critical theory within an interview with Gurnam Singh in June 2008 as being 'cobbled together' from a variety of different traditions including Marxism, feminist epistemologies, and anarchistic work. Amsler (2013, p.198) does however differ from the views of Giroux (1983) with regard to critical theory being a 'school of thought' in that she clearly states 'It is not a form of neo- Marxism or a tightly paramatised school of thought, as the Frankfurt School of critical theory is sometimes mistakenly misunderstood.' Amsler (2013) proposes that critical theory is more about human experiences and relationships which can be subjected to critical analysis in order to enlighten our understanding as to the causes of social injustices and ultimately the realisation that these situations do not have to be permanent or unchanging.

In addition Amsler (2013) also considers that critical theory can provide the tools to enlighten our understanding of the links between societal factors such as culture, political forces, physical bodies and consciousness in order to challenge powerful relationships and structures. Once these processes of enlightenment have become disclosed Amsler (2013) suggests that there are possibilities to transform subjective and social life experiences. Amsler (2013, p.198) states clearly and succinctly that 'For me, critical theory is an interdisciplinary way of knowing the world that is orientated towards both understanding and improving it'.

Critical and Transformational Teaching Styles, the Influence upon Students

Freire (1996) explains how critical thinking and transformational teaching practices aim to help individuals to gain a sense of agency and become active in order to work towards transforming their own society. This transformation occurs as a result of gaining literacy and critical thinking skills which in turn leads to heightened levels of self-awareness. Freire felt that dominating ideologies prevented individuals having a clear view as to how this had an effect upon their own lives. Freire (1996) also proposes that individuals adopt a 'naïve consciousness' based on a fragmented view of reality and partial explanations as to why behaviours and actions become accepted within society. As a result of these distorted ideologies oppressive practices are maintained and become the status quo (Darder, Baltodana and Torres 2009).

Freire, (1996) also suggests that critical thinking involves debates about issues of culture and personal aspects of reality. Freire (1996, p.104) considers that 'As they discuss the world of culture, they express their level of awareness of reality, in which various themes are implicit. Their discussion touches upon other aspects of reality, which comes to be perceived in an increasingly conscious manner. These aspects in turn involve many other themes.' Within this research the participants were given the opportunity to voice their opinions about their own themes and versions of reality with regard to their own educational experiences. The participants were then encouraged to consider other wider sociological themes, such as oppressive and dominating power structures within society.

In order to avoid the resulting alienating effects associated with the banking style of teaching, my students are encouraged to openly discuss their life experiences in relation to the sociological topics they study on the course. The need and desire to discuss and contextualise their life experiences is something that students have told me has helped them to see where their versions of the 'real world' have been engendered and produced.

The encouragement of critical thinking can be thought of as both a practical way of helping individual's to become aware of alternative strategies to enhance personal agency, and a theoretical teaching practice by raising awareness of dominant power structures in society. It is my contention that an increased level of political awareness of oppressive power structures arising from this type of teaching practice can have a practical consequence in terms of personal agency. This contention was addressed within the research with consideration to the participants' prior experiences of a banking style of education, as 'passive student's (Freire, 1996), as opposed to the transformational teaching practices they experienced at the Riverside East College.

During discussions in teaching sessions it has become apparent that as Undergraduates the realisation of how previous life and educational experiences have shaped their version of reality can be quite unsettling for them as adults. These feelings of discomfort increase even more for most of them when they start to think critically and question the validity of previously held beliefs and 'established' knowledge. Although these feelings can be uncomfortable, the students have reported that by questioning their own status quo they have been 'transformed and enlightened' gaining a sense of freedom to think for themselves. In Chapter Four (Research Findings), and Chapter Six, (Conclusions), the reported quotes demonstrate as to how and why the students began to question their previously held beliefs and knowledge of 'facts'. Unfortunately however for some individuals, transformation can bring with it associated risks and a fear of freedom (Fromm, (1961), Freire, (1996) hooks, (1994).

Critical and Transformational Teaching Styles, the Influence upon Teachers

Understandably, perhaps, Freire and Shor (1986) acknowledge that there are also fears for teachers who teach in a liberating pedagogical style rather than that of established and traditional teaching methods. These fears are associated with their employing institutions and their careers, as a more critical thinking, and transformative teaching style may run the risk of disapproval from their employers, especially perhaps if working within a neoliberalist environment. Freire and Shor (1986) discuss the fear that teachers may have in terms of risking a demonstration of their professional skills in front of their learners if they use an experimental teaching practice. In addition the teachers may find that their learners prefer more traditional styles of teaching in order to gain the knowledge they consider necessary for future employment prospects. In this respect Freire; (1998, p.41) proposes that 'When we are faced with concrete fears, such as losing our jobs or of not being promoted, we feel the need to set certain limits to our fear. Before anything else, we begin to recognise that fear is part of being alive'.

It could therefore be suggested that there may be an element of fear and anxiety for both teachers and students undertaking critical teaching and learning if students are allowed to actually influence and shape their educational experiences by gaining a voice. The fear that may be associated with the teacher having to evaluate and question their own expertise, and a fear of losing their teaching confidence, employment prospects, and for the students there may be a fear of not learning in a manner that will facilitate their assessments and future qualification.

The black feminist author bell hooks (1994) writing in the tradition of transformational teaching practices talks of how teaching can 'transgress' traditional and male dominated teaching in Universities, and as such can bring about criticisms and sanctions. hooks (1994) also suggests that students and educators should be encouraged to take risks and share their narrative life histories in order to produce a sense of empowerment for everyone and enable academic theories to be applied to real life experiences. In this manner hooks considers that teachers will not be reinforcing dominant ideologies, or work from a position of power and domination themselves. Although the experience of sharing life experiences within the classroom may open up feelings of vulnerability for educators, by taking these risks hooks (1994, p.21) proposes that they will be 'wholly present in mind, body and spirit'. hooks (1994) also suggests that the classroom will become an environment for resistance and that everyone will gain a voice and recognition for their contributions to the learning process.

Bovill (2011) provides practical advice as to how students can gain a voice and take responsibility for their own learning, and learning from their peers by using evaluation to reflect upon their own contributions to class discussions. Bovill (2011) works in a practical manner, practicing in the field of critical thinking with Undergraduates by helping the students to learn through critical analysis, and self-reflection regarding their own contribution to learning.

Bovill (2011) proposes that by using practical initial evaluation exercises such as 'stop/start/continue' developed by George and Cowen (1999) students can actively help to influence the teachers teaching practices. Students are asked to report what they would like the teacher to 'stop' doing, and what they would like them to start or continue to do. The students are then asked to evaluate their own contribution to learning by evaluating what they believe they should stop, start and continue to practice within class. By using this type of practical exercise Bovill (2011, p.99) proposes that:

'Evaluation of teaching and learning has the potential to facilitate teacher and student reflection on both teaching and learning. This implies evaluation based on a partnership model where dialogue between academic staff and students is the heart of decisions about adaptations and innovations in teaching and learning. This reflects a Freirean view of shifting agencies within the classroom from the 'teacher-of-the student's and the 'student- of- the teacher' towards new roles he has defined as 'teacher-student and students-teachers.'

As teachers and students alike can contribute to the shaping of the practical manner in which teaching and learning takes place, Bovill (2011) proposes that everyone has a responsibility for evaluating the teaching and learning experience and as a result the potential to shape the learning experience. Bovill, Cook-Sather, and Felten, (2011, p. 25) also propose that 'Having the opportunity to work collaboratively with faculty in developing pedagogical approaches inspires students to experience an increased sense of engagement, motivation, and enthusiasm'. In addition Bovill et al. (2011) also consider that the teachers gain a great deal of enthusiasm and a sense of re-invigoration and a 'renewed commitment to learning.' Bovill, et al. (2009, p. 25) quotes a teacher who states that after teaching in a collaborative interactive style it 'really transformed how I think about teaching and how I teach. And the buzz I get from teaching in a way that's interactive…it's really changed how I work'.

The benefit of students influencing and having an impact upon their learning experiences, does however remind 'students of the social nature of learning and the value of learning from peers…and opens a dialogue about learning and teaching with academic staff…as well as how different teaching approaches can impact upon, and influence learning' Bovill (2011, p.101).

Although it can be considered laudable to give students a voice via different exercises and the demonstration of critical thinking skills, these exercises can instil another type of anxiety for teachers regarding the national publication of the annual National Student Survey (NSS) scores. Bovill (2011) considers that student learning experiences reported in surveys such as the National Student Survey (NSS) can provide some evidence of how students evaluate their teaching and learning experiences.

This type of measurement is not however without its critics (Beecham, 2009). Healey, Flint and Harrington (2014) propose that performance measures such as the NSS scores in the UK give more credence to statistical quantifiable outcomes, rather than creative processes, which I consider, are more associated with dialogue and critical thinking processes. I also consider that the use of quantitative statistics such as the NSS scores do not capture the overall learning process experienced over the 3 years of a Degree experience. As the surveys are usually conducted in March and April of the 3rd year, they only provide a limited snapshot of the students views prior to the completion of the teaching experiences.

At Riverside East College, NSS scores usually yield very high levels of satisfaction for the sociology course, which is the subject of this research. The scores usually range from 92% satisfaction to 100% which is obviously pleasing for the Social Science Team. There are, however, potential problems with this type of measurement in that with student numbers usually around 20/25 for each year, statistically if only one student indicates they are not satisfied with their teaching and learning experiences the results can be considerably skewed and as such not representative. If the NSS results are skewed in this manner and indicate that there has been a drop in student satisfaction, the Social Science Team would be held accountable for this. Clearly the possible consequences for HE in FE teachers is likely to engender feelings of fear and anxiety as their future employment opportunities may be under threat, which supports the arguments raised by Freire and Shor (1986), Fromm, (1961) and hooks, (1994).

It would seem therefore, that a sense of fear is clearly associated with the human experience of teaching, but by giving the students the opportunity to have an empowering voice as part of the NSS process, there are risks and feelings of anxiety associated with this exercise for teachers. Bovill (2011) proposes that a more effective method would be to encourage dialogue between the teacher and students by critically evaluating their own contribution to learning throughout the course of the programme. At the Riverside East College students discuss their own contribution to the learning process during seminars and tutorials on both an individual and group basis. These discussions also tend to follow feedback given after assessment processes, during which the tutors and students discuss the contribution they have both made to class discussions and research.

Critical and Transformational Teaching, the Relationships between Teachers and Students

Freire (1996) makes it clear that there is a need for a 'problem solving' type of education which necessitates the use of critical thinking, through dialogue and interactions between the teachers and students. The boundaries between what might be called a teacher and the learners should be broken down within these educational environments as according to Freire (1996, p.53) who states, 'Education must begin with the solution of the teacher-student contradiction, by reconciling the poles of contradiction so that both are simultaneously teachers and learners'. The influence and impact upon teaching practices and research, as a result of the dialogue between teachers and students is further explored by Eaton (2015), who considers that this form of relationship dates back to Wilhelm Humboldt at the beginning of the 19th century. In this respect Eaton (2015) proposes that the history of student's being involved in communities of research is therefore founded in history, and as such is 'nothing new'.

The manner in which education has been taught within Universities in the USA was a powerful medium for promoting and sustaining issues of oppression and supremacy according to hooks

(1994). The need to change this promotion of oppression could therefore only be achieved within learning communities by confronting and challenging academic perceptions of truth in terms of white male supremacy. The idea of confronting these historical assumptions of teaching practices that hooks termed as safe, was however likely to cause a certain amount of panic and unrest within the classroom. hooks (1994) refers to fear in terms of how educators would view these challenges to the historically established teaching methods which did not allow for this type of confrontation or lack of conformity. hooks (1994, p.33) states: 'We cannot be easily discouraged. We cannot despair when there is conflict. Our solidarity must be affirmed by a shared belief in a spirit of intellectual openness that celebrates diversity, welcomes dissent, and rejoices in collective dedication to truth'. Regretfully however, within an even more contemporary neoliberalist society since hooks made this statement and one that encourages individualism rather than solidarity, this could be a problematic ideal to work towards.

The question as to what it means to work within a community of learners, for both students and teachers is addressed by bell hooks (1994) who considers that she discovered learning could be a revolutionary experience at her all black children's school. During her childhood experiences at school, hooks suggests that she always felt teachers 'knew' their pupils well in terms of knowing their parents and economic status. It also seemed that the teachers had often taught the whole family who would have historical ties with the teachers. This historical knowledge of pupils seems to reflect Freire's concept of knowing his students 'intimately' within a learning community.

In order to build up a trusting relationship within the classroom hooks (1994) proposed that all students should feel acknowledged and valued. Furthermore the contributions from the students should be thought of as a valuable resource generating excitement within the classroom. Excitement should take place within the classroom hooks (1994) for any pleasure or beneficial learning practices to occur, although this should not be the sole responsibility of the teacher but will be dependent upon the mutual interactions between all group members. This notion of all group members producing a collective learning experience in order to form a community and avoid the banking system is clearly a reflection of Freire's philosophy of radical pedagogy Freire (1996) hooks (1994).

A study by Healey, Flint and Harrington (2014) reflects the work of Freire (1996) hooks (1994) regarding communities of learners, and clearly resonates with my Research regarding critical teaching practices, student and teacher relationships. Healey, Flint and Harrington (2014) research is written with a political focus upon current 'wider economic factors', and the need to challenge teaching practices which may engender passive, rather than active learners. Healey, Flint and Harrington (2014, p.7) propose that:

> 'Engaging students and staff effectively as partners in learning and teaching is arguably one of the most important issues facing higher education in the 21st century ... Wider economic factors and recent policy changes are influencing a contemporary environment in which students are often positioned as passive consumers of, rather than participants in, their own higher education'

As within this Research the exploration of how prior teaching practices concerning passive consumers of education may be associated with the banking system of education and the current political influences, this statement rings true. By contrast the transformative teaching practices the participants have experienced at Riverside East College are thought to have motivated them to be 'active' in their own development of learning. Rather than passively absorbing a 'hidden curriculum' that has been imposed upon them, they have been given the opportunity to actively question and critically assess the reliability and validity of traditionally accepted 'facts' and knowledge.

Although Healey et al. (2014, p.7) acknowledge that there are a multitude of other factors in which students and staff can work together as 'partners' the emphasis in their research is that 'partnership represents a sophisticated and effective approach to student engagement because it offers the potential for a more authentic engagement with the nature of learning itself and the possibility for genuinely transformative learning experiences for all involved'. Furthermore, Healey et al. (2014) propose that it is only through the process of students and staff working together, and learning together that a true sense of an authentic engagement can be achieved for everyone. When referring to an authentic engagement, within my own Research I take the stance that an authentic engagement not only applies to teacher and student relationships, but in addition an engagement with an authentic version of reality regarding the humanisation of the curriculum, as opposed to a sterile acquisition of traditional educational beliefs that support the banking style of teaching (Freire, 1996).

At the Riverside East College the Undergraduate Dissertations are developed and researched by the students with very little teaching of factual material, or 'deposits' (Freire, 1996) as each person is working on their own unique research topic. These students have however, already been taught for almost three years in a critical teaching style involving a great deal of dialogue between themselves and the Social Science teachers within informal tutorials for this final assessment. As a result of these interactions both students and teachers learn a lot from each other and between them create and produce new knowledge. The creation of this new knowledge produces a synthesis of work, which has been developed through the student's autonomous agency and critical thinking processes, and the discussions with the teachers. The Undergraduate Dissertations are therefore considered examples of current, developmental and meaningful creations of knowledge for individuals living in their own version of reality, which is also grounded in critical theory.

The final year dissertations also indicated how the students have become more aware of injustices within wider society, as they have often chosen topics that relate to contemporary issues that they consider need to be addressed and acted upon. In this manner the effects of the transformational teaching in the class room they have experienced, has been demonstrated. The chosen projects were also usually associated with issues they wanted to be employed in following the completion of their degree. The student employment aspirations also demonstrated their enhanced desire to instigate change, through their own sense of agency.

In addition Healey et al. (2014) consider that a community of teachers and learners engagements and relationships are not solely linked to one particular project or learning experience. The engagement process continues beyond one or two learning experiences to form a partnership and community of learners that is likely to be sustained over a period of time. 'Partnership is more likely to be sustained where there is a strong sense of community among staff and students. The key to achieving this is the development of *partnership learning communities*' (Authors Healey et al. (2014, p.8) own emphasis in italics). In this sense, all of the participants, both learners and staff, in this research have formed a type of learning community over a long period of time, of at least 2 years and up to 20 years. The relationships between the learners and staff have certainly been sustained in this respect, to the extent that some of the former students taking part in this research are now teachers and teaching in a transformative style themselves.

The familiarity and relationship of the teachers and learners is explored further within this Research, in order to contextualise the teaching practices of HE Sociology within Riverside East College. Within the community of learners at the College it is thought that the participants feelings of trust in their teachers has helped them to gain the confidence necessary and take risks to engage in challenging critical thinking dialogues, which again supports the conclusions made by Healey et al. (2014, p.7) who consider that:

> 'Partnership as a process of engagement uniquely foregrounds qualities that put reciprocal learning at the heart of the relationship, such as trust, risk, inter-dependence and agency. In its difference to other, perhaps more traditional, forms of learning…partnership raises awareness of implicit assumptions, encourages critical reflection and opens up new ways of thinking, learning and working in contemporary higher education. Partnership is essentially a process of engagement, not a product'.

As to what is meant by a community of learners is also addressed by Amsler, et al. (2010) who question what this terminology actually means. Furthermore, as to whether a virtual community of learners is possible in the absence, or reduction of face to face interactions is raised by (Amsler, et al. 2010). The question of possible virtual communities is a matter of consideration for Amsler, et al. (2010) regarding the need to develop strategies and possibilities for collective action when necessary. At the Riverside East College I consider there is what I would describe as a community of learners. My students who are working and interacting with their peers and lecturers within this community have demonstrated their power to challenge senior management decisions when necessary. It is difficult to imagine that without face to face interactions within their community of learners these challenges would have been so effective.

As the majority of students studying on the course at the Riverside East College are female and working class, it was thought that the work of bell hooks was particularly relevant to the theoretical framework and the review of literature. In addition as the Riverside East College is an FE College providing HE, rather than a University, I consider that a 'learning community' (hooks, 1994) has been established. In this sense there is a great deal of emphasis given to the need to maintain a sharing and supportive working environment between the teachers and learners. Although clearly there are some necessary power relationships and boundaries between the teachers and students, every effort is made to ensure that everyone is treated in a respectful and equal manner.

Pedagogy of Fear

As this research is written in a somewhat innovative writing style this has brought about a personal 'fear of freedom' for me. Within this review of literature I have given a great deal of consideration as to how Fromm, (1961), Freire (1996), hooks (1994), and Freire and Shor (1986) talk of the fears and risks associated with transformational education. In order to be congruent with the key critical thinkers associated with this research, however, this is a risk I was prepared to take in order to relay my own developing and enlightened transformational experience as a teacher and participant within this research.

Freire was influenced by the work of Fromm (1961) among others who argued that with all attempts to become emancipated from oppression and personal changes in life there is a fear of freedom that has to be overcome in order for an individual to be liberated intellectually and as such become transformed. Fromm was born in

1900 in Frankfurt Main Germany and worked as both a sociologist and psychoanalyst, which ironically are the same disciplines I teach. Fromm was clearly influenced by Freud, and stated that he had a deep respect for him, as well as Karl Marx, which again ironically are two individuals I teach my students about in great depth. Fromm's work is often described as being anti-authoritarian and non-conformist, which clearly links to both Freire (1996) and hooks (1994). Fromm is also thought of as being a leading proponent of critical thinking having taught at the Frankfurt School. Originally the Frankfurt School comprised of Marxist's who considered that Marx's theories underestimated the extent that individuals were affected by 'false consciousness'.

Fromm, (1961) proposes that if an escape from an established reality occurs the individual can feel distanced from cultural and social norms that have been embedded on a deep psychological level. Fromm, (1961, p. x) states that 'Freedom, though it has brought him independence and rationality, has made him isolated and, thereby, anxious and powerless'. At Riverside East College students have reported that if they plucked up enough courage to voice a different viewpoint to that of their peers or teachers during their school educational experiences, they felt anxious and a sense of isolated from the group. It would seem therefore that this fear of moving away from established reality ensured these individuals were more likely to succumb to other powers of authority and oppression. Fromm, (1961) links the fear of freedom and feelings of powerless to reasons as to why individuals may become associated with Fascism and Nazism. Psychological mechanisms of escape which individuals develop to escape reality ensure that 'in our effort to escape from aloneness and powerlessness, we are ready to get rid of our individual self either by submission to new forms of authority or by a compulsive conforming to accepted patterns' (Fromm, 1961, p.116).

Fromm's, (1961) somewhat gloomy and deterministic viewpoint of how an individual can be transformed in an attempt to escape from the fear of reality is reflected within Freire's (1996) teachings. Freire (1996, p.27) states that 'during the initial stage of the struggle, the oppressed, instead of striving for liberation, tend themselves to become oppressors, or 'sub-oppressors'. Freire (1996) seems to suggest in this respect that initially men, in particular, have become so indoctrinated and dehumanised by their oppression they believe to oppress others is part of their own role in life, a normal and natural behaviour for them to continue with. Furthermore it is also necessary to adhere to the people who have oppressed them within a position of safety, albeit unpleasant, rather than risk an unknown situation, where a person could feel isolated and cut off from their own version of established reality.

There is however a great deal of difference for individuals when they achieve 'conscientization' and a level of awareness of their own oppression. Freire, (1996, p.26) does however offer hope for humanity who have been 'dehumanised' by oppression by stating that 'to admit of dehumanisation as an historical vocation would lead to either to cynicism or total despair. The struggle for humanisation, for the emancipation of labor, for the overcoming of alienation, for the affirmation of men and women as persons would be meaningless'. For Freire therefore it would seem that although there would be a struggle, it is possible for humans to break free from oppression, but that this struggle for freedom 'must come from the oppressed themselves and from those who are truly solidary with them' (Freire, 1996, p.27).

The desire to seek freedom from their class and gender issues of oppression can often initiate a sense of fear (Fromm, 1961) associated with breaking away from the familiar socialisation patterns embedded within my student's early educational experiences. I have become fully aware of this sense of fear in my students, and indeed myself as a working class female when initially undertaking studies at Degree level. This sense of fear is usually demonstrated by a lack of confidence and a naïve, state or media indoctrinated belief that if something is written in an academic book or through the media these are facts that are true and, therefore, there is a legitimacy of both the author and the performer. The Undergraduate Degree programme I have helped to develop and teach on for almost twenty years is associated with critical thinking and as such questioning traditional established 'facts' that have been taught and socialised, which can for some initiate a sense of fear. I have, therefore, addressed this question of fear of freedom by including the work of Fromm (1961) in this review of literature.

Pedagogy of Hope, Freedom, and Transformation

Savin-Baden, (2013, p.23) states that Marx's work 'focused on transformation and he suggested that social theorists and underprivileged people alike should strive for revolution and social change'. These Marxist concerns are pertinent to this current research with particular consideration of social change becoming possible rather than determined without any hope of a more democratic society and transformation. The ability to influence change and challenge dominant ideologies, particularly those associated with effects of neoliberalist practices in education is addressed by Amsler et al. (2010, p. 12) who consider one of their aims is to:

> 'Challenge the individualised atomisation and instrumental and fatalist thinking that Neoliberalism encourages in part through its assumption that 'There is No Alternative' (TINA). We, in contrast, seek to create learning and teaching environments in formal and informal educational spaces that facilitate dialogue, reflexivity and connection to real life needs that enable the creation of methodologies encouraging and realising more democratic practices'

This statement reflects the aims of my research and the methodology of looking at the responses to semi structured interview questions, in order to explore whether the participants consider that as a result of their educational experiences they can become agents of change in connection with themselves and society. The manner in which everyone can become agents of change and challenge capitalist domination and oppression in the 'real world' is addressed by John Holloway (2010).

Holloway (2010) reflects the need to challenge educational practices (McLaren, 2006, Freire, 1996) by considering that one way of 'Cracking Capitalism' is through critical teaching and raising levels of awareness and agency in students. Holloway (2010, p.23) proposes that:

> 'The cracks are not always a direct spill-over from more limited struggles. Sometimes they arise from a conscious decision of a group of people to reject the constraints of capitalism. It may be a group of students who decide that they do not want to subject their lives to the requirements of capitalism and will find a way of living against and beyond the system as far as they can'.

Holloway (2010, p.23), does however acknowledge that individuals do not always make a conscious attempt to reject capitalism power structures and may instead experience an 'expulsion from capitalist social relations. More and more people are being pushed out of employment or finding that they have no way of becoming employed at all.' Holloway's proposal with regard to unemployment seems to reflect Fromm's (1961) and Freire (1996, p.17) viewpoints regarding the fear of freedom. If people fear they may risk unemployment, this will help the educational neoliberalist forces to maintain and expand a workforce that does not necessarily experience an awareness of oppressive power structures. In addition if students choose to study at institutions where critical thinking practices are prevalent, they may not experience the same employment opportunities, and as such risk unemployment, which again would favour the capitalist forces in that as Holloway (2010, p.23) suggests 'The state systems of unemployment benefits... are designed to extend the discipline of employment even to the unemployed, to make sure that the unemployed really function as an industrial reserve army of labour'.

This 'no win' scenario is not one that critical thinkers working together can, or will contemplate, and it is certainly not the stance I take in terms of my conceptual framework and teaching practices. My intention is to adopt the political participation advocated by John Holloway in Crack Capitalism (2010), and Freire (1996). In this respect I consider that the teaching practices at the Riverside East College can help to initiate and engender the cracks within the capitalist and neoliberalist forces that attempt to reduce the availability of critical thinking courses in FE and Universities. Holloway uses the terms 'our', 'we' and 'us' liberally throughout his text to emphasise the importance of the participation of ordinary individuals, like me a Sociology HE lecturer working in an FE environment, to produce cracks in capitalism. Holloway (2010, p.3) also makes it quite clear that the need for participation from ordinary people is a matter of urgency- 'Break. We want to break. We want to break the world as it is … we refuse to submit our lives to the rule of money… There is urgency in all this.'

Holloway provides a stirring account as to how political participation and forms of peaceful rebellion can 'Crack Capitalism'. Holloway (2010) also provides practical advice as to how political activity can work towards a peaceful and urgent revolution and produce cracks in capitalism which according to the author are 'obvious' and achievable. Holloway (2010, p.04) states 'There is nothing special about being an anti-capitalist revolutionary. This is the story of many, many people, of millions perhaps billions'. Holloway then goes on to list several examples of the types of people who can work towards producing cracks in capitalism including (2010, p.04) 'the University professor in Athens who creates a seminar outside the University framework for the promotion of critical thought ... it is the gardener in Cholula who creates a garden to struggle against the destruction of nature ... the book publisher in Barcelona who centres his activity on publishing books against capitalism'. In this sense I consider that I could be added to this list which would read something like: 'The UK Sociology HE Lecturer who encourages Undergraduates through critical teaching practices to challenge the capitalist status quo and realise their own agency within society.'

Overall it would seem therefore that 'ordinary' people in different walks of life can produce the changes necessary for working towards the reduction or indeed destruction of capitalist domination. Holloway (2010, p.06) also looks at how individuals can appear to be very different in that they are united and 'share in a movement of refusal-and-other-creation: they are rebels, not victims; subjects, not objects.' So for Holloway one of the routes to emancipation is to stop creating tyrants by stopping working for them and serving them. Holloway does however state that for many people this is very difficult as the consequences could be poverty, starvation or in the most extreme cases torture and death. Holloway forcefully addresses the point that many people have failed to produce revolutions because society is so entrenched into capitalism it seems hopeless to resist.

So the question is then, what can we do about it, - if as according to Holloway the answer is obvious and simple? Holloway (2010) provides a very obvious and simple solution which when pointed out makes the reader aware as to how ordinary people can help to crack capitalism. Quite simply the solution is for everyone to enter into the process of some cognitive restructuring which basically means that we stop thinking of capitalism as a 'wall' that cannot be damaged or knocked down permanently. Holloway (2010) suggests we look for the cracks in the wall of capitalist domination, and consider the inner conflicts and weaknesses within this system rather than thinking it is hopeless to even try and bring about change.

Holloway (2010, p.09) states 'The method of the crack is the method of crisis … This is crisis theory, critical theory … Critical/crisis theory is the theory of our own misfitting. Humanity (in all its senses) jars increasingly with capitalism.' This statement clearly supports the notion of the Common and the Commons

(Roggero 2012, Neary 2013). The dichotomy and conflicts between the natural world and the ever increasing demands of the socially constructed world of capitalism is succinctly stated by Holloway's (2010, p.09) proposal 'That is the basis of our cracks and the growing importance of dialectic of misfitting'.

I also consider that there is a 'misfit' between my student's desire for transformational education and their traditional working class traditions at the Riverside East College, especially for the female Undergraduates. Within the rural 'natural world' where the Riverside East College is situated the male students relate how they have been encouraged to seek permanent employment working on the land or other rural jobs, which are low paid and reflect working class traditional roles. The females in particular relate how their previous educational experiences were transmitted by teachers who promoted traditional gender roles associated with low paid, temporary employment until they get married and have children. For both the female and male participants, therefore, little or no encouragement to gain, or indeed produce living knowledge was given within their early educational experiences at school, according to the discussions held with the sociology Teaching Team. The students have also stated within class discussions that their working class traditions and roles have been challenged by the critical thinking and teaching practices at the Riverside East College.

In the following Chapter Three, the qualitative methodology used in this research demonstrates how teaching practices have influenced the participants' views of their class, gender, and sense of 'reality' both within and outside of the classroom. Furthermore the extent that the participants have gained an enhanced sense of oppressive educational practices, or by contrast, feelings of agency and transformation are addressed within the participants' narratives and responses to the semi structured interview questions.

Chapter Three Methodology

Introduction

This chapter deals with the overall design of the research, showing how the qualitative methods address the Research Questions. The relationship between ontology and epistemology within the research is also demonstrated with particular reference to my own class and gender to the critical importance of reflexivity within the research. The factors taken into account when designing the research approach, such as the selection of participants, interview and data collection and coding procedures are also considered within this chapter. The manner in which the structure of the research ties in with the methodology and transformational teaching practices is linked to the '3 stages' associated with Freirean principles (Sweet, (1998). The purpose of this chapter is, therefore, to demonstrate the relationships between the review of literature, methodology and transformational teaching practices within the classroom.

The Overall Research Design

The research design was reflected upon throughout the study as Bogdan and Taylor, (1975), cited in Cresswell, (2007, p.5) proposes 'By *research design,* I refer to the entireprocess of research from conceptualising a problem to writing research questions, and on to data collection, analysis, interpretation, and report writing'. The research design and analysis of the narratives and the sharing of personal viewpoints within the interviews, was styled to gauge whether key sociological concepts such as class and gender had been an influential factor concerning their perception of educational experiences. Furthermore as apart from one, all of the participants including the teachers, considered themselves as coming from a working class background, the research methodology provided information as to whether interactions between themselves and their teachers have been influenced by the lack of the social barriers of class.

The design of the semi-structured interviews and questions provided opportunities to explore class issues associated with the interactions, the familiarity of the teachers, and the learning environment of an FE college. Furthermore, as the teachers themselves considered they were working class, rather than middle class, with the associated norms and values, the interview questions and responses provided opportunities to see whether similarities of social background were influential in terms of critical teaching practices, and the generation of a shared, similar version of a constructed reality.

The Research Approach, Qualitative Semi-Structured Interviews

The method for obtaining information for the research was semi-structured interviews incorporating narrative life stories and a discussion of teaching practices. The research approach provided participants with opportunities to talk freely and informally about their educational experiences from both a historical and current perspective. The open questions gave the participants opportunities to reflect upon their own varied experiences of HE educational experiences. The students and teachers accounts of their life stories

117

and their educational experiences informed the research by providing links between the theoretical framework covered in Chapter Two and the practical experience of studying upon the same programme, in the same institution, and being taught in the same transformational teaching style.

Justification for the Methodology

The work of Jenkins, Canaan, Filippakou, and Strudwick, (2011) was considered particularly relevant to my research in terms of, both the methodology used in their research and my own. These authors set out within their article the benefits and the justifications of using auto biographical methods. In my research, I am using narratives, including my own, within semi-structured interviews in a similar manner. Jenkins et al. (2011, p.7) discuss the merits of using auto-biographies as a 'pedagogic tool and consider autobiography to be an epistemological concept concerned less with what is written about a life or by whom than with different ways of writing/visualising and describing lives.'

The justification for using narrative accounts and semi structured interviews was to provide a new and innovative methodology that incorporated dialogues from participants, including myself, and a comprehensive review of literature of critical thinkers working in this field. In this respect I considered that the methodology developed and used in my research produced an appropriate qualitative research method to explore transformative teaching practices, and add to the body of existing literature concerning critical thinking approaches. The literature written by Koro-Ljungberg and Greckhamer, (2005) is supported by Cresswell (2007, p.3) who states:

> 'some researchers have called for a methodological dialogue to address questions of disciplinary power, theoretical future of the field, alternative theoretical approaches, discontinuance of conceptual traditions, new methods of training and preparation, and alternative writing and publication possibilities.'

Stuart (2012) highlights the benefits of using life histories as a methodology in order to understand social changes in society especially in terms of class and education. As this research explored who or what is responsible for life's inequalities within a neoliberalist society the life histories supported the work of Archer (2003). Stuart (2012) suggests that American sociological studies have always been interested in life history work although the research methods were usually associated with case studies in general.

Historically studies such as Becker (1970) Plummer (1975) and Thompson (2000) have involved interviewing people about their life experiences in order to bring meaning to social changes in society according to Stuart (2012). Rustin, (2000, p.34) as cited in Stuart (2012) states: 'it is not surprising that a new focus on individuals is having an influence on the methods in the social sciences. In such a climate the time seems right for a methodological turn towards the study of individuals, a turn to biography.'

The use of life histories and narratives concerningthe participants' educational experiences was therefore considered totally appropriate for qualitative research. Stuart (2012, p.28) succinctly provides clear support for this type of method by stating that 'The life history approach provides a both richness and level of understanding that cannot be gained from survey data because it is at the heart of the individual's experience'.

The justification for using the semi-structured interviews regarding narrative life stories was that the methodology linked explicitly to the research problem. By studying the narrative information from the participants' perspective a true and realistic picture arose regarding the notion of HE education. In particular the subject discipline of sociology was thought to provide a form of specific enlightenment with regard to whether it is possible to challenge capitalist dominated systems which may regulate how people are educated.

As narrative life stories can be obtained from a variety of mediums to produce an individual's life account it inevitably provided a great deal of rich and relevant information. The semi structured interviews provided information in the form of spoken and recorded narrative life stories and questions from all of the participants.

Justification for the Methodology Factors taken into account when Designing the Research Approach

As the research problem, methodology and questions were focused upon teaching practices the actual content of what was taught was considered to be a factor. Although the research reflected upon transformational teaching styles, which is not necessarily linked to one particular discipline and as such interdisciplinary, the robustness of the methodology was enhanced by focusing on one discipline (sociology) at one level (Undergraduate) in one type of teaching and learning environment (HE in an FE institution).

Participant Selection and Rationale

There were 27 participants in the research, consisting of 20 females and 7 males which reflected the higher ratio of females on the course. As the course is populated with more females than males with a variety of ages between 18 to mid-60's the selection of participants reflected these demographic characteristics. The youngest participant was aged 18 and the oldest (a previous student) aged 66 years.

The sample of participants included all 7 of the current members of the Social Science Teaching Team, five current students in the first, second, and third year of the course and five previous students who have already completed the course. The participants volunteered to take part in the research as a result of a poster displayed within the teaching area of the Riverside East College.

The invitation to participate attracted more participants within the sampling frame than needed. The selection of participants was restricted in numbers and justified in that I wanted to be guided by the work of Freire (1996) and hook's (1994), in terms of working within a close knit 'community' of learners. As the course attracts several students who actually know each other, through friendship or a relationship within the rural location of Riverside East College they have had several opportunities to discuss the teaching and learning practices within the classrooms, or within the social environments outside of the college. As such I considered that as the participants share and hear each other's narratives about internal and external aspects of their current and previous educational experiences, they can be thought of as a community of learners which exists both within the classroom and the external environment. The manner in which I have categorised the participants as a community of learners reflects hooks (1994, p.186) who states:

> 'Hearing each other's voices, individual thoughts, and sometimes associating these voices with personal experience makes us more acutely aware of each other ... Sharing experiences and confessional narratives in the classroom helps establish communal commitment to learning. These narrative moments are usually the space where the assumption that we share a common class background and perspective is disrupted'.

Justification for My Own Role as a Participant in the Research

As an active participant in the research, I responded to the same narrative and semi structured questions asked of the other teachers within a staged interview with a colleague. My responses to the interview questions were spoken aloud, and then immediately typed up by a touch typist. The full written transcript of the responses were used to generate data, and considered within the analysis of the Research Questions (included in Chapter Four Data Report). (The full transcript of my interview responses within my role as a teacher is included in the Appendix section). My participation in the research interviews were considered of prime importance as it provided a clear justification for the use of qualitative methods as Mason (1996, p.5) considers,

> 'Qualitative research should involve self- scrutiny by the researcher, or active reflexivity. This means that the researcher should constantly take stock of their actions and their role in the research process, and subject these to the same critical scrutiny as the rest of their 'data'. This is based on the belief that a researcher cannot be neutral, or objective, or detached, from the knowledge and evidence they are generating. Instead they should seek to understand their role in that process'.

In addition my own role as a participant, and the data generated, provided evidence of my own positionality and ontology when developing the research design. My own data and written transcript demonstrated how my views of the social world influenced the research. Clearly my data supported the points made by Mason (1996) and proved to be very influential, in that as a researcher my own life experiences are directly responsible for my ontology.

Furthermore as the research was influenced by my own positionality concerning how the data was collected and generated, the qualitative methodology of the semi-structured interviews demonstrated my epistemology.

The Pilot Interview Procedures

In the initial and exploratory pilot interviews the participants were told about the Research Questions, and asked about their prior educational experiences in education, but not given any specific questions or prompts. Although the narratives were interesting, and respectfully listened to, they lacked focus, and did not address the research questions in any depth. The 3 participants talked a great deal about being personally transformed by the critical teaching techniques they had experienced, and their feelings of an increased sense of agency. However, the responses given addressed individual and personal relationship changes, and their accounts of leaving abusive partnerships, and acceptance of their sexual identity for example. As a result of these individualised and personal accounts, a semi structured interview schedule was developed, providing open questions about educational experiences and prompts. The revised interview design resulted in gaining data concerned with more shared, focused educational experiences, rather than individualised very personal accounts. The inclusion of sociological keywords and topics such as democracy and oppression engendered a more focused discussion of teaching practices rather than transformational, personal experiences in the individual's lives.

The Consolidated Interview Procedures

The selected 27 participants were interviewed at the Riverside East College during mutually convenient times on the days when they were due to be in attendance. The interviews lasted for up to one hour each. Written, and or oral information and consent to record the responses was gained from the participants prior to the commencement of the semi structured interviews.

Following a review of the literature the following Open, Interview Questions were generated:

1. 'Tell me about your experience of education since leaving school please?'

2. Tell me how teaching practices have impacted on your learning inside and outside of class – in a positive and negative way.

3. What are the key themes/ideas that have emerged for you from these learning experiences?

4. I have a list of words that describe the themes I think are important regarding student learning experiences which I would like to share and discuss with you. But before we discuss these themes would you rank them in order of what you think are the most important please?

(1 being the most important and 6 being the least important)

Alternatively please feel free to mark any words that you feel are not important as N/A (Not applicable)

My words describing the themes are:-

Democracy, Oppression, Equality, Freedom, Transformation, Enlightenment

5. Please clarify as to why you chose which of the themes as being more important than others

6. Please tell me how have the experiences of being a student in your classes affected how you see yourself as a student, in terms of your role and student identity

6TP. Can you tell me how have the experiences of being a student in these classes affected your teaching practice?

As can be seen, the Interview Questions for the teaching team participants were identical to those asked of the current and previous student participants with the exception of the last question (Q6) which was replaced by Q6TP (Coded for Teacher Participants). At the conclusion of the interview all participants were asked if they had any questions and then thanked for their participation in the research. Participants were also informed that they would be provided with a typed account of their interview upon request.

Data Collection procedures

All of the information gained from the semi structured interviews was digitally recorded. The recording of the interviews provided opportunities to listen to them repeatedly and thus ensure high levels of validity and accuracy when transcribing the accounts and the consequent coding processes. In addition, the digital recording of interviews produced 'raw data preserved in a verifiable form' (Walker, 1985, p.110). The information gained from the participants was prepared for analysis by using the following qualitative research methods:

All of the interviews were audio recorded

All of the semi structured interview data were transcribed

The transcripts were coded in order to produce summarised data and original key quotations.

Coding and Analysis of the Information gained from the Narrative Interviews

The narrative interviews and qualitative data gained from the transcriptions were subjected to extensive in-depth coding and analytical procedures. The manner in which the data was coded for the research followed the patterns proposed by Saldana (2009) in that in the first instance the data was given a descriptive code for sections or key words taken from the transcribed interviews. Key words or phrases that had not been anticipated or expected were also noted in the first cycle of coding.

During the interviews Question 4, (key words/prompts) associated with critical teaching practices and the Undergraduate's key subject matters in sociology were introduced. Responses to these key words and the hierarchal levels of importance given by the participants were subjected to coding and consideration. The aim of this process was to give consideration as to whether the teaching practices the

Undergraduates experienced had impacted upon their own attitudes of empowerment and agency within the classroom and their everyday lives.

Adler and Adler (1987) suggest that the manner in which data is coded is intrinsically linked to the researcher in terms of the personal involvement and perceptions of the researcher. Within this research the life narratives of the participants was considered to be of key importance as having an influence upon how the data was gathered and coded. The coding of the data was therefore dependent upon considerations of the class, and gender of all participants, including that of myself. The coding process of class and gender resulted from the responses gained from the semi structured questions.

My positionality within the research was considered crucial regarding the manner in which the information was generated and coded in that I have been teaching the same course within the same institution for a period of twenty years. During this extensive period of teaching I have been aware that students repeatedly refer to the manner in which they have been taught as being a crucial factor in their learning experiences. The emphasis given to the teaching practices the student's experienced, at Riverside East College has inspired the Research.

Environmental factors, such as the Teaching Environment and the Learning Landscape, and the familiarity of the teachers prior to studying on the Undergraduate course, have been voiced every year as having a clear influence on the students learning experience. Several opportunities were, however, given to the participants during the narrative interviews and open questions to offer alternative and differing viewpoints. It was thought that any unexpected responses to the open questions would help to produce new and innovative teaching practices of HE in FE institutions. It was also thought that the unique manner in which the research combines several influential factors, such as prior experiences of education, and reflections of identity, added to and enhanced the existing theories concerning teaching practices. In this respect the narrative interview responses produced opportunities to generate and code the data in an inductive manner.

The information gained and the manner in which it was coded and analysed was dependent upon factors such as the comprehensive review of the literature, and my positionality as a teacher, researcher and participant. These types of judgemental procedures are supported by Saldana (2009, p.07) who states 'All coding is a judgement call' since we bring 'our subjectivities, our personalities, our personalities, our predispositions (and) our quirks' to the process.'

Coding Cycle 1 Descriptive Factors

The tables which demonstrated the following descriptive factors below in the Cycle 1 coding process can be found in the Appendix Section:

Table One,   Key descriptive words or phrases

Table Two,   Anonymised participants' names

Table Three, Interview Question 1 (Q1) prior educational experiences

Table Four,   Interview Question 2 (Q2) impact of teaching practices

Table Five,   Interview Question 4 (Q4) key words prompts responses

Table Six,   Interview Question 4 (Q4) overall summary of responses

Questions 3, (key themes) Question 5, (importance of key words), Question 6, (student identity), and Question 6TP (influence upon teaching practice) are not demonstrated in a tabular format due to the more thematic nature of the responses (Coding Cycle 2)

Cycle 2 Thematic Analysis

The qualitative data gained from the narratives and interview questions were subjected to thematic and in-depth, analytical procedures to look for particular subjective themes and feelings arising from the participants learning experiences. The thematic insights into the transformational effects were explored by the interpretation of their discourse and use of key words throughout the discussion. By giving the participants the opportunity to reflect upon their experiences, and then actually discuss these experiences throughout the interview, it was considered that they would become even more aware of their own perceptions of their identity as agents of change. As Freire (1996, p.68) proposes:

> 'As we attempt to analyse dialogue as a human phenomenon, we discover something which is the essence of dialogue itself: *the word.* But the word is more than just an instrument which makes dialogue possible; accordingly, we must seek its constitutive elements. Within the word we find two

dimensions, reflection and action, in such radical interaction that if one is sacrificed – even in part- the other immediately suffers. There is no true word that is not at the same time praxis. Thus, to speak a true word is to transform the world'.

Key Words

Within the interview Question 4 (key words prompts responses) the participants were provided with 6 key words/prompts which emerged from the Review of the Literature concerning transformational teaching styles. Responses to the key words and the hierarchal levels of importance given by the participants generated from Interview Question 5 (importance of key words), were subjected to analysis and explicitly linked to the Research Questions. The responses to Interview Question 6 (student identity), from the student participants and Q6TP (influence upon teaching practice) from the teacher participants were analysed subjectively and thematically with regard to their accounts of personal and practical transformational changes that occurred as a result of their teaching and learning experiences.

Metaphors (Code MM)

In addition to the initial coding processes another code (MM, Meaning of the Metaphors) within the narrative interviews, was produced. It was thought that the exploration of the metaphors would provide additional clarity as to the thematic meaning behind the actual words used during the interviews.

Processing of Information

All of the anonymous recordings were stored in computer files which could only be accessed via hidden passwords. All recordings were made available to the University of Lincoln academic staff for assessment purposes on request. The processing of the information gained from the taped interviews was transcribed and any notes taken were made available to participants and for assessment purposes if required. All participants were given an opportunity to amend or delete any information supplied from the interviews if requested. My own reflexive narrative life story was produced within the data collected and subjected to analysis and self-reflection. The information gained from the participants was interpreted by the identification of key words, patterns of educational experiences, and general sociological themes such as class, race and gender. Patterns of consistency and themes emerging from the narrative life stories were observed and considered during and after the interviews.

The theoretical underpinning of the research, the Research Questions, and the review of the literature conducted prior to the interviews provided an expectation as to the patterns that would emerge from the information gained. Stake, (1995, p.78) suggests that these prior expectations provide a 'template for the analysis'. It was also acknowledged that these prior expectations may be challenged and contradict the key concepts associated with this research in that one or more individuals may have had a single significant experience that shaped their educational experiences. The context of the Teaching Environment and the Learning Landscape, at Riverside East College, the subjectivity of the experience and patterns that arose provided a robust and valid methodology.

Ethical Considerations

With regard to any ethical power relationship considerations, it was acknowledged that it was difficult to maintain a completely equal power relationship between the teacher and student (Freire 1996) or in this instance participant. Consideration to power relationships was given, as within the Riverside East College my usual role is that of a teacher, rather than that of a researcher and interviewer. Students were however informed that within the Riverside East College permission had been given to conduct the voluntary participant interviews based on the principle of a mutual agreement rather than a lecture based session, which addressed the issues surrounding power relationships. In addition the current Undergraduates were interviewed during periods when they were not being formally assessed in order to avoid any responses given as being influential concerning the grading of their future work.

Standard Ethical Procedures

Clearly with any research ethical considerations are of paramount importance, Jenkins et al. (2011) consider that for their students ethical issues are clearly addressed within the student's dissertations, research and theoretical considerations within their studies. This is also the case with my students throughout the three years of their studies. Students are asked to provide written evidence of ethical considerations, such as participant consent and information sheets when conducting any of their own empirical research. In a similar way to Jenkins et al's (2011) study, all of the participants, including myself were aware of the paramount importance in adhering to ethical procedures within my research. The relationship between the sociological studies associated with class having real meaning for the participants involved, like Jenkins et al. (2011) the question of ethics was reflected upon both by the development of the research design and the conducting of the narratives and semi-structured interviews.

Every individual was informed that they were able to withdraw their information and participation from the research at any point. As this research was thought of as ongoing and developmental, the reasons as to why a participant might wish to withdraw may enlighten any future work regarding critical and transformative teaching practices and narrative life experiences. If any participant had preferred not to discuss the reasons for wishing to withdraw their information I would have provided an exit interview if desired.

If I had needed to acquire any further training for interviewing the participants there were facilities to do this at the Riverside East College. I also had the support of my supervisors at the University of Lincoln. Written ethical approval from the University of Lincoln had been gained prior to the interviews and the collection of data commenced. Written permission from the Riverside East College had also been gained prior to the interviews and the commencement of data collection. All of the participants had been informed that anonymous accounts of their educational experiences would produce data concerning learning and teaching experiences for the EdD qualification and publication. As the research was a developing and on-going project, ethical considerations were constantly reviewed in light of any new issues that might have occurred.

The structure of the research with regards to the methodology, positionality of the participants, and theory, were directly linked to the critical thinking teaching practices as reviewed in the literature (Chapter Two). In recognition of my own developing 'conscientization' and 'praxis' (Freire, 1996), after reviewing the literature again I realised that the research methodology clearly reflected the two stages of Freirean pedagogy. Freire (1996, p.36) described the two stages as:

> 'In the first, the oppressed unveil the world of oppression and through praxis commit themselves to its transformation. In the second stage, in which the reality of the oppression has already been transformed, this pedagogy ceases to belong to the oppressed and becomes a pedagogy of all people in the process of permanent liberation. In both stages, it is always through action in depth that the culture of domination is culturally confronted'.

Sweet (1998) expands upon Freire's stages to outline three stages, which although virtually identical in content, clearly sets out a logical structure as to how a state of 'the culture of domination is culturally confronted' can be achieved. In this respect, the research findings have been linked to these three stages, which have given an appropriate structure for the analysis of the findings, and the conclusions drawn from the research. According to Sweet (1998), Stage one is quite simply the recognition that as individuals they have been subjected to oppressive practices. Stage two involves understanding the grounds for their oppression, and Stage three involves actually doing something about it in order to counter that oppression.

Stage One–Raise the Awareness of Oppressive Practices (Interview Question 1)

With regard to my positionality, which is explicitly entrenched within this research, I considered that my Undergraduate sociology studies enabled my journey through Stage one. I soon began to recognise the hegemonic and dominant power of working class educational traditions for females through the discussions with my teachers and peers studying Undergraduate sociology with me. The manner in which I put these stages into practice within the methodology and interview questions are demonstrated as follows.

In my teaching and within the research I considered I raised the participants' awareness of oppressive practices with reference to their previous educational experiences. By requesting participants to 'tell me about your educational experiences since you left school' (Interview Question 1), I gave them opportunities to recognise how, or indeed if, they have been subjected to oppressive educational practices.

Stage Two-Understanding the Grounds for Oppression (Interview Questions 2/3)

As my educational journey progressed and I studied feminist theoretical approaches, and Marx, Freud, and Fromm in particular, I reached Stage two and started to realise how and why I had been educationally oppressed. Although I do not feel that this stage has reached a logical conclusion that can be thought of as 'done and dusted'. As part of my current educational experiences, and within my role of an educator myself I consider I am in a perpetual state of Stage two, constantly learning established and contemporary

141

grounds for oppression such as neoliberalist effects in U.K Universities today.

Stage two was addressed within the research by exploring whether the participants understood the possible grounds for their oppression by asking 'tell me how teaching practices have impacted on your learning inside and outside of class – in a positive and negative way' (Interview Question 2). In order to focus down more as to whether the participants had recognised through their learning experiences what particular grounds of oppression they had experienced I asked them 'What are the key themes/ideas that have emerged for you from these learning experiences?'(Interview Question 3)

Stage Three–Teaching Practice, Prompts and Agency (Interview Questions 4/ 5)

After I achieved the dizzy heights of becoming a Sociology Undergraduate teacher I became aware of how I had gained a certain amount of agency through my transformational teaching approach. I began to see how I could help my student's journey through Stage one and Stage two, and as such I began my journey through Stage three, by actually doing something about challenging ruling class hegemony and traditions by teaching in a critical and transformational style.

The interview questions 4 and 5 were used to explore the extent transformational teaching experiences had raised an awareness of oppressive practices, both inside and outside the classroom, and a sense of agency to challenge these practices. Within the interview question 4 the participants were asked to rank the themes and key words (Democracy, Oppression, Equality, Freedom, Transformation, and Enlightenment) as generated from the review of the literature. The key words were chosen in order to demonstrate themes of oppression, and a sense of enlightenment of this with particular reference to their own circumstances.

Within question 5 the participants were asked to clarify why they chose some of the themes as being more important than others. This was done in order to explore their perception as to whether they could actually do something to challenge social inequalities, as agents of change. The responses given were monitored so that I could see whether they thought there was no alternative to social inequalities, or opportunities possible to actively work towards instigating changes. The monitoring of the responses to the questions 4 and 5 related to the Critical and Transformational Teaching Styles, and the influence upon students addressed in the review of literature.

Oppressive Power Structures of Class and Gender issues, how Critical thinking helps to engender a sense of Escape from Oppression (Interview Question 6)

The overall aims of the research were addressed within question 6, when the current and previous students were asked 'have the experiences of being a student in your classes affected how you see yourself as a student, in terms of your role and student identity'? This question generated responses pertaining to their awareness of the banking system of education, usually at school, and how this affected their version of 'Reality' and Dominating Ideologies. In this respect, issues of class and gender in particular were monitored as to how this affected their sense of identity. Furthermore, question 6 was used to generate responses from the current and previous students, to see if they had gained an increased sense of agency as a factor associated with their sense of identity.

Transformational Teaching Styles, Influence upon Teachers, Relationships between Teachers and Students, Pedagogy of Hope (Interview Question 6TP)

Again the overall aims of the research were addressed in this question, although this question was directly aimed at the teachers. This question was asked in order to explore whether the effect of being a student at the Riverside East College had influenced their own current teaching practice, and as such, generate another group of critical thinking individuals. Within the research an exploration of the relationship between each generation of teachers and students was considered crucial in order to instil a pedagogy of hope, and feelings that an escape from oppressive practices in education was possible. For the teachers, question 6 TP was used to demonstrate their sense of agency, and transformation to Stage 3, e.g. to see if they were 'actually doing something' to challenge oppressive power structures, by teaching in a critical, transformational style themselves.

Transformational Teaching- Critical Theory and Practice in the Classroom.

A central aspect of this thesis is transformational teaching practice so I would like to describe my transformational teaching methods. I have been inspired by the theoretical work of Paula Allman (2010). From reading an account of her teaching practices I can see that there are similarities and differences between our approaches to teaching. The first similarity with Allman's work at Notting University and my research became apparent when I read of her desire to, 'apply or translate Paulo Freire's philosophical approach to critical education within a specific context that was entirely different from that of Freire- one that many would deem an inappropriate context for his approach to critical education' Allman, (2010, p.173).

The context of my teaching and research was also 'entirely different' to Freire's work, both in location and time period, as was Allman's teaching in an English University, whereas I am teaching in an FE College. There were however similarities between Allman, (2010), and Freire, (1996) and my research in that there was a profound belief that teaching could never be done from a 'neutral viewpoint' and was therefore inherently political, and as such has transformational effects including a sense of agency, upon both the teachers and learners.

Allman, (2010, p. 173) describes her account of the application of Freire's work as being 'based on my personal memories and critical reflection' although she did keep diaries of the research which helped her to 'refocus and reflect on what happened during the day'. I have also kept critical, reflective, and reflexive notes throughout the process of conducting this research, and recording my teaching practices, both from the teacher's viewpoints and the learners .As I have written about this research in a humanised style, I have also been reliant upon reflecting upon my 'personal memories', and that of all the participants.

In Chapter Six, the conclusion, I have shared these personal memories and reflective thoughts with you the reader, and like Allman (2010) linked the theoretical work I have covered in Chapter Two to the teaching practices we use at theRiverside East College. What follows next in this Chapter is a review of how I and the other teachers use a Freirean educational approach to demonstrate how:

'The entire process is important … Freirean education cannot possibly work by imposition … we were doing as much as we possibly could to assure ourselves and the entire learning group that we were all committed, at least in principle, to trying to learn together in an alternative, unconventional and what we hoped would become a revolutionary way' Allman (2010, p. 178).

Transformational Teaching – how we do it at the Riverside East College

As the HE teaching for the course takes place in an FE College rather than within a University setting we are somewhat restricted to what we teach in that certain core, compulsory modules are pathway specific. We do however as a team have the ability to choose which of the optional modules we want to teach, in order to make up the credits necessary. To a certain extent therefore the compulsory modules we have to teach has restricted our power and agency within the learning environment, due to allocated learning outcomes, assessment formats, teaching hours and the time span for each module. By contrast however, there are no real constrictions as to *how we teach,* which gives us the academic freedom to use transformational teaching practices. (These issues of empowerment and agency for the teaching team directly relate to the Research Question 3 and question 6TP, teaching practice).

With consideration as to how we actually teach in a transformational manner, the first question that arises is, apart from earning a living, and making sure the students are able to successfully complete their assessments, we have to ask what the purpose of our teaching is? As academics we feel that scholarly activity, and the desire to inspire and motivate our students to want to learn is the reason, rather than any political or capitalist rewards. We also know what our purpose is not, which is the Banking Style of education Freire (1996) and all teachers teaching in a transformation style, are so opposed to. Or as one new teacher, not teaching on the Undergraduate sociology discipline told me, her purpose was to 'drill in the facts' to A Level students, in order that they pass their exams, an issue which can be associated with the fear of teaching. So having established that we are not restricted to teaching in a Banking Style, sometimes referred to as 'Information Teaching' we are not 'teaching by numbers' as Vincent (3TTV) so aptly spoke of.

Indeed we are in a way 'working backwards' from the Banking Style, as we start off not by 'drilling in the facts' and information, but in contrast we ask the students *what they already know* about the topic, and we ask the students to 'teach us' and give us their version of reality in terms of the subject. We do this by having little group discussions, followed by a whole group plenary, involving everyone having a voice. We then return to the small groups and ask them to think about *why* they have informed these opinions, which usually is met with the response such as 'we were taught it at school, or my parents and grandparents have always said...' We then have the basis for an in-depth discussion as to how there could be another way of looking at what they consider to be established facts, or traditional viewpoints usually associated with their class and gender.

One way the teaching team have found of challenging traditional belief systems, and generating a sometimes heated discussion, involving critical thinking, is to quote a highly controversial statement made by someone who is in total opposition to the need to be aware of, or challenge social injustices. Sometimes we will quote racist, sexist or fascist public figures, which although it makes us as teachers feel very uncomfortable saying the words; it also makes the students feel not only uncomfortable, but anxious, and usually outraged too. The uncomfortable, anxious feelings generated in this manner have the effects related to the Stages of transformational teaching talked of within this research, Freire, (1996) and Sweet (1989).

Firstly the students start to think about *why* they may consider that women should be housewives or mothers, rather than academics, for example (Stage One, interview question 1). Secondly, they start to think about *why and who* might be transmitting this viewpoint, so in this example the response might be, 'well Dad always wanted his dinner on the table when he come home from work and he said that after all that was women's work'. Which although this proposed response seems very much at odds with what might be considered contemporary roles within the family, sadly the reality is that unless, or until individuals become aware of these forms of oppression, these power structures can remain unchallenged, and the status quo maintained. By bringing the reasons why oppressive forces are in place through the processes of critical thinking, (Stage 2) feelings of agency are enhanced and the students start to question what they can do about challenging this form of dominating ideology (Stage 3).

As the discipline of teaching sociology is obviously associated with historical, current, and fears of future oppressive power structures, the teachers and students are able to relate to issues that they have been personally involved in, such as gender and class issues for example. So another way we teach to transgress against 'established facts', and traditional informational teaching, is to engender a desire to challenge these 'facts'. By using the close and trustworthy relationship between the teachers and students, we share anecdotal, real experiences of how, as a small learning community, we have been affected by these dominant power structures. In this way we start to build upon our multiple versions of reality, and become more aware as to why we hold these views, both as individuals and as members of the wider society.

In order to contextualise our versions of reality in terms of 'the world', both inside and outside of the classroom, I often relate the example as to how, as working class females just starting work in a huge office of clerical workers, my friends and I experienced the lunch hour in the work's canteen. I tell the students how the male employees were in the elite minority, so they had an area cordoned off for their exclusive use, whereas the females being in the less favoured majority, sometimes had to stand up to eat their dinner, even though there were empty seats in the exclusively male section.

This true example of gender discrimination always sparks off feelings associated with enhanced levels of awareness, critical thinking and agency. The students then provide their own examples and a version of reality associated with the topic, and a lively debate and discussion always follows.

In order to provide some balance to the debate however, I give the example of how my husband was spoken to by the bank manager in charge of our meagre economic resources. When he found out that my husband was unable to work due to long term health problems the bank manager in his position of power said 'well you have got a cushy life having your wife working to support you'. This remark clearly demonstrated that he thought gender roles were specific, and that the man was duty bound to oppress the woman by providing the resources to 'keep her'. By using this example I think the students become more aware of gender oppression, and that it is not necessarily exclusive to females, but may be associated with working class values as well. During, and following these discussions, the students are then able to develop and produce contextualised, social constructionist arguments associated with both theory and the real world, or as Freire considered, the humanisation of the curriculum.

For two of the social construction modules I teach, I have a lot more power and agency in that I am the only person who teaches them, either in the franchised University that validates the Degree or the other Regional FE Colleges teaching the other sociology modules. I do therefore work quite intensely with the students to develop the essay questions that they think are most appropriate to address the topic, Psychoanalysis and the Self. We also agree to have an 'open question' which as long as it is in tune with the level of module, and can be thought of as appropriate, and realistically possible to work upon within the time span, is acceptable. By giving the students the opportunity to choose the essay titles they find the work exciting, as hooks suggests work in the classroom should be, and furthermore they consider the topic area in terms of their own versions of reality and life experiences, all of which provides them with an enhanced sense of personal agency.

As there is an additional 'in class test' for the first year version of this topic, again, we work together to decide what the questions should be, and how we can relate these to contextualised, topical and contemporary situations. We do therefore select an episode of a popular 'soap opera' and devise questions around it. Although it could be suggested that the version of reality demonstrated in a soap opera involves some highly unusual and unlikely circumstances, such as dramatic or emotional traumas for individuals happening on a day to day basis, the soap opera portrays 'a version' of possible life experiences. A soap opera episode is used to aid the learning process due to ethical considerations, as obviously a discussion and analysis of people personally known to them would be totally unethical. Furthermore the students would not have, or be expected to have the professional skills necessary to be able to work with individuals needing psychoanalysis. This appreciation of ethical considerations was closely adhered to within this research by ensuring that all names and the learning environment was anonymised and processed in a confidential manner.

When the students sit the test therefore they are fully aware of the questions and the foreseen information, but in order to answer them they have had to be involved in how and why they chose them, and researched the theoretical underpinning basis. As this is a the first year of Undergraduate study module, I consider this formative learning process for an in class test, has far greater implications for developing critical thinking styles, rather than memorising the isolated segments of information necessary to answer questions in a formal, unseen exam. I also think that whoever writes the formal exams is in a position of power, and exclusive types of knowledge, that do not necessarily fit with the versions of reality of working class students. Which I suppose, brings us to ask again what is the purpose of teaching and scholarly activity? Is it to do with the transmission of exclusive facts, or to encourage critical and transformative thinking?

Although clearly as Undergraduates their subjective versions of reality will not suffice for assignment purposes, we then have to follow up the discussions with further debate and encourage the students to research and demonstrate which theory or literature might support their ontological position, or by contrast opposing views. This process is something I have done by researching the available and existing literature in the review of literature (Chapter Two) in this research. Indeed as I have been writing up the process as to how we teach in a transformational manner, I have gained an enhanced level of awareness and effectiveness of my own teaching practice, and my confidence in the trustworthiness and justification of this research.

As a result of writing up this segment of the research I have given consideration to the Research Questions by looking at how the underpinning theoretical concerns are associated with transformational teaching. I have also written this report in a humanised style, talked about the methodology of how we actually 'do something' to address class and gender oppressive examples, and as such worked through all of the Stages associated with transformational teaching. In this manner I think I have produced a reflective, reflexive and summarised analysis of the whole Research, and each Chapter included in this Thesis. Perhaps it is fitting therefore that this section represents how this research adds to the existing knowledge of Transformational Teaching, both in theory and actual Practice.

In the following Chapter Four the main findings that arose from the interview questions are generalised and supported by direct quotes taken from the participants' voices and responses. The key findings were then directly related to the Research Questions, with consideration to the effects of transformational teaching practices upon both students and teachers. The findings presented in the following Chapter Four are also contextualised to the learning landscape at Riverside East College, and the research problem as considered in Chapter One.

I invite you the reader to join me now to see how I am actually 'doing something' to show how this research, and my 'voice' and those of the other research participants have travelled through, and continue to travel through, the Freirean stages (Sweet, 1998) which are reflected in the findings.

Chapter Four Research Findings

Introduction

The information given during the semi structured interviews provided rich, robust information regarding the effects upon both teachers, and learner's educational experiences and teaching practices.

In order to produce a logical and well-structured review of the research findings an overview of the responses gained from each of the interview questions was produced. The responses gained from each interview question were then explicitly linked in a narrative form to the Research Questions, and the two stages of the 'humanist and libertarian pedagogy' Freire, (1996, p.36), and the contemporary adaptation to three stages, Sweet (1998).

In some instances, tables were produced, (which can be found in the Appendix Section) to demonstrate the descriptive responses gained as part of the first stage of coding. The responses gained from this cycle of coding, and the data gained from the second cycle of coding are reported within an in-depth thematic analysis in the following Chapter Five.

Overall Summary of Initial Key Findings for Each of the Interview Questions

The findings for each question are supported by quotes from the participants, followed by a summary for each question with consideration of the main points.

Interview Question 1; tell me about your experience of education since leaving school please?

Within the first cycle of coding (Appendix Three), Table Three was produced to indicate the descriptive points made by the participants regarding their previous educational experiences. As can be seen from these descriptive findings, the participants indicated that they viewed their educational experiences at school in a very negative fashion. Furthermore, several of the female participants narrated that their educational experiences were explicitly linked to their gender expected roles, as daughters, mothers and wives. It would also appear that the participants were not necessarily aware of how they may have been oppressed by their prior teaching and learning experiences (Stage one). For Roxy and Joan it seemed that they either had no knowledge of the importance, or the possibility of attending University as a result of their home or educational experiences.

Roxy (23PSR) reported that she was brought up in a single parent family with a father '*who was very negative...you're rubbish, you can't do that...although I was always in top groups and if I sat a test I'd do really well but I never completed the course work side of things and that would bring my mark down... we were latch door kids- your cleaning and your cooking came first... I didn't realise how important education was then'.* As Roxy (23RPS) is a fairly young student I was surprised by her comments as her viewpoints and that of her father's could be contextualised to the 1950's era in the UK.

Joan, (27PSJH), who came from a working class background, attending a local rural school, clearly expressed the view that her future career choices were limited, and that she was not given any encouragement to attend University. Furthermore it seemed that none of her peers were encouraged to either follow an academic route, indeed, by contrast Joan talked about how most of them went into apprenticeships rather than University.

'My education was very local, I went to school ... which was only 15 miles up the road and one of the things I found most about going to school ... was that there was absolutely no encouragement for aspiration, so I was given a very stark choice that I could be a typist, because there were no computers in school when I was in school, but we did have lots of typewriters ... So I came to college and learnt typewriting and got a distinction, so I was an outstanding typist, but I knew that was not something I wanted to do and because of the fact that there were no aspirations ... So I actually left school and came to College ... but still no one, even here gave any indication that, that could lead to anything else. There was never any discussion about University. In fact nobody I knew went to University, even those that were in the top stream went into apprenticeships and have got very good jobs from them, but nobody that I went to school with went to University. So, some even became Actors, but no one went to University. So I drifted basically because of that' (27PSJH).

Interview Question 1, Summary

- Gender issues raised more for teachers than students

- Age Issues tended to be more of a factor in terms of youth or context (epoch)

- Previous Teaching and Learning experience very positive in terms of Access Course

- Previous Teaching and Learning experience very negative (School with comparison to latter experiences)

- Familiarity of tutors more of a factor for Access students (prior learning) taught by same HE Social Science teachers

- Pastoral Care more of a negative factor for Teaching Team (referring to school /prior to learning experiences on Degree)

- Not Applicable (N/A) responses given ambivalent, or participants unable to remember with what they considered accuracy

Interview Question 2; tell me how teaching practices have impacted on your learning inside and outside of the class – in a positive and negative way

Within the first cycle of coding (Appendix Four) Table Four was produced to indicate the key points made by the participants regarding the impact their teaching experiences upon the Degree programme had upon them. As can be seen from the 2 quotes below their responses indicated that they had become more aware of the oppressive and powerful structures within society (Stage 2).

'I'm definitely, more critical, analytical of life, people's motives, just life in general. I definitely view things differently, even turning on the television; it's the reasons behind why they are showing that story when there are other bigger stories out there. Are they trying to take our focus away and that sort of thing? (15Y2W).

'From the Degree I was able to articulate what I had always believed, I had always believed that the world was unequal and unfair and that inequality was based on money- and through my studies- and engaging with Marx's theories I was able to understand that for me economic determinism is fundamental to understanding inequality' (27PSJH).

Interview Question 2, Summary

- All participants - aimed their responses at the research Degree Programme (1TTJ -refers to my own Undergraduate experience)

- All participants - positive responses given regarding impact of teaching practices in classroom on the Degree programme at Riverside East College

- All participants - positive responses given regarding impact of teaching practices outside of classroom dependent upon subjective interpretation of researcher e.g. more critical. Participants also made several references to the 'world' which indicated an increased awareness of how the teaching practices had impacted upon their belief systems outside of the classroom

- All participants - positive responses regarding impact of teaching practices in life overall- dependent upon subjective interpretation of researcher e.g. more radical

- Most participants felt there had been no negative impacts upon their overall life in general

- Some participants felt that after experiencing the teaching practices they were constantly questioning everything – which did not allow them to 'switch off' from the current or prior discussions in class

- Some participants felt that after experiencing the teaching practices they were constantly questioning everything - a positive impact dependent upon subjective interpretation of researcher e.g. argue more

- Key words most frequently used were: confidence, empowerment, enthusiasm, critical, questioning, the world

- Teaching Practices upon the Degree were considered in a very positive manner as opposed to the very negative comments made of prior experiences at School as stated in Question 1

Interview Question 3; what are the Key Themes/ideas that have emerged for you from these learning experiences?

The three groups of participants provided responses to question 3 as demonstrated below by a selection of typical key sentences and the key words used. A summary of the edited extracts of findings is provided at the end of the responses to Question 3 in order to provide insights into the general thoughts and feelings expressed by most of the respondents. All of the participant responses are written in italics to demonstrate that they are direct quotes. As the examples expressed below are considered representative of most of the participants it is envisaged that these extracts will give a general 'flavour' of the responses and provide a sound basis for the analysis of these key findings in Chapter Five.

All of the Teaching Team responses were included in the form of quotes as it was considered necessary to demonstrate their positionality, including my own, with regard to their teaching practices and the manner this may have had an influence upon the students perception of social issues, agency and transformation. These issues will be expanded upon in a lot more depth within the thematic analysis of results in Chapter Five as being totally salient and key to the Research Questions.

Fuller, longer and more contextualised responses from the current and previous students were given in order to provide the basis for the in depth analysis in Chapter Five. As the research aimed to explore whether teaching practices had a transformational effect upon the current and previous students, it was considered necessary to contextualise the responses to Interview Question 3 within the general demographic nature of the students and the FE Riverside East College itself. The personal and individual effects the teaching practices have had upon the student's families and everyday lives are demonstrated within these longer quotes.

'I suppose the key things from my working class background, my education and teaching practices is that you have to fight to bring about the changes you want' (1TTJ).

'I think I always had a passion for political ideas and social change and that wasn't really reflected in school as we didn't really do a lot of that … I don't feel that the education system encouraged that' (2TTS).

'I won't just accept the sort of things that are just told by the media, - I challenge things out there…now even looking at some of the broadsheet papers, you look through the content and you can see there is a definite political bias and they are using it to achieve some goal' (3TTV).

'Until I did the Degree, I didn't realise how gullible I was ... it didn't occur to me that because it wasn't in the news, it didn't go on ... I'm not gullible now... I've opened my eyes more to what goes on in the world' (4TTJS).

'One of the main things that I took away from the Degree was that knowledge and awareness of Society and the desire to kind of pass that on. It is kind of life changing and you're eyes are opened... It's like an Epiphany- definitely one of the main things I took away from the Degree, that, and the confidence to be able to express those ideas as well' (5TTD).

'I could really see ... how actually society is just a result of a lot of powerful institutions exercising power ... that did affect me personally, improving obviously my general understanding, my sociological understanding and as a person an understanding of myself' (6TTL).

'I had felt unfulfilled and quite unhappy and then coming here the pieces just fell into place ... I think the content is quite thought provoking, but its more than that, it's so much more than that' (7TTC).

'Everything is about perception – me and my boyfriend- we had this disagreement – his Dad started on that capitalism is great ... so I pulled that to pieces after the lesson we had with Saul ... Then he said I don't like Saul with all these ideas - I do not think he hates him – but it's just these ideas' (9Y1L).

'I do question a lot more, which I think is a positive thing. I actually feel as though I was very blinkered before I started the course. You just listen to what you're told, this is how it is, but it's a bigger world out there and there's a lot more going on behind the scenes and this course has made me question it- definitely' (15Y2W).

'As the Degree got more and more intense the way I observed life changed ... The biggest one was my job ... then I started getting introduced to Marx ... and I started understanding human emotions behind it all and I started looking at the way it was run and I started thinking that this is more an organic machine rather than a place where human emotions are understood and are recognised ... It also helps me understand the impact of feminism and equality ... It feels like a freedom ... It's like someone opening a door and you walk through it ... and see that not everything is as simple as it's been made out to be' (18Y3C).

'It gave me was the confidence to know that criticism of Marxism is through fear and it's through not understanding- or upholding a system ... but when you study Marx historians, they are not slaves to Marxism they are exploring an absolute valid idea and for me that's what was empowering because I realised that what I had always believed actually, the system was unfair and the system was unequal and we were living a lie and that was not conspiratorial, it wasn't a conspiracy, it was actually evidence based ... so I was actually able to articulate that in recognising that the government was engaging in a policy of divide and rule that was very pernicious and very persuasive' (27PSJH).

Interview Question 3, Summary

- The Teaching Team responses indicate that they are clearly critical of the media and its influence upon societal attitudes and belief systems

- There is evidence of an in depth political awareness associated with the Teaching Team individuals which has had an influence upon their students

- The Teaching Team participants demonstrated their agency and desire for change

- The student participants had clearly been influenced by the political aspects of the course and their teachers

- All participants demonstrated how their sociological knowledge gained was applicable to real life and was not just theoretical concepts

Interview Question 4; I have a list of words that describe the themes I think are important regarding student learning experiences which I would like to share and discuss with you. But before we discuss these themes would you rank them in order of what you think are the most important please? (1 being the most important and 6 being the least important) Alternatively please feel free to mark any words that you feel are not important as N/A (Not applicable). My words describing the themes are: Democracy (Q4D) Oppression (Q4O) Equality (Q4E) Freedom (Q4F) Transformation (Q4T) Enlightenment (Q4EL)

This question involved asking participants to respond to 6 key words (prompts) and then list them in a hierarchical order as to what each key word meant to them personally. The prompts used were generated by the review of literature as being the key words that were consistently associated with transformative teaching practices. The ranked numbered responses is demonstrated in Table Five, (Appendix Five) and summarised below in terms of descriptive numerical data within these initial coding procedures.

Interview Question 4, Summary

The Prompts Ranked as Most Important was:

- The highest number of 1's was Enlightenment (14)

- The second highest number of 1's was Equality (11)

The Prompts Ranked as Least Important

- The highest number of 6's was Oppression (15)

- The second highest number of 6's was Democracy (5)

The none representative examples of ranking the themes

- The two participants (1TTJ) and (27PSJ) who considered all of the key words (prompts) were of equal importance and ranked them 1, were both sociology/history teachers

- Two participants considered some of the key words (prompts) were not realistic and ranked them N/A

Interview Question 5; can you clarify as to why you chose some of the themes as being more important than others?

The responses gained from Interview Question 5 gave participants an opportunity to express their views succinctly with regard to how the teaching practices effected how they viewed key sociological factors within society. Interview Question 5 was considered a particularly useful exercise in terms of providing a sound basis for the thematic analysis of the Research Questions in Chapter Five.

Due to the fullness and comprehensive nature of the responses to Interview Question 5 edited extracts from each of the participant groups are provided below. The participants' accounts reflect the overall responses given to this question. Within the following Chapter Five (Data Analysis) selected sentences and phrases from the participants were used to illustrate how the generated data linked to the review of literature, theoretical concepts, methodology and the conceptual framework applied to the research. All of the participant responses are written in italics to demonstrate that they are direct quotes.

174

Democracy

'Democracy is a wonderful idea and one that I hope one day everyone in society will recognise and accept, unfortunately, in order to be totally democratic, the rich and powerful people would have to make sacrifices and I am not sure that is ever possible, so it is a wonderful idea, but in reality I am somewhat pessimistic that it will   ever   happen,   -   true   democracy' *(1TTJ).*

'Democracy is a nice ideal but it doesn't exist in any country in the world ... I remember reading about Ghandi when he was brought over to England and they said to him 'what do you think of democracy in England, Mr Ghandi?' and he said 'I think it would be a good idea!'- I don't think anything has changed' (2TTS).

'Democracy, there is no real democracy; I don't feel - because I don't feel it's particularly important in my classroom there is no

democracy ... I am a tyrant because I make them listen to me and I make them think, they don't have a choice' (5TTD).

'Democracy's a lost claim, I think ... Democracy is fake to me, you get your own choice but you're picking from someone else's ideas' (17Y2C).

'Democracy is absolutely important to discuss but in terms of real democracy, not the kinds of democracy that we have been taught and that we live within, because I don't believe we do live in a democratic country, I believe that we live in an oppressed country where we are fed the fact that we are free and we are democratic and actually we are not' (27PSJ).

Oppression

'As an adult, I now realise that oppression can be something that is not only about physical elements, but more importantly perhaps it is about the oppression of mind as well' (1TTJ).

'I teach people about oppression through capitalism and several other methodologies in our societies. But oppression is only something that occurs if you allow it to. No one can be oppressed unless they give their permission ... when it comes to brute force, people submit not through their own volition but simply through

176

fear. So there is no real power as such, except for the fear and if you can conquer the fear then you can conquer oppression' (2TTS).

'I don't agree with oppressive regimes, whether it's in the classroom or in the organisation, I don't believe you can achieve anything through that, it restricts ideas, it restricts thinking, it restricts creativity. It's something we try and challenge and get people to think about so that they can challenge oppressive ideas and beliefs and maybe look at the wider world' (3TTV).

'Oppression – is something I have experienced a lot of ... after studying with Saul I know I was an oppressed functionalist. I know my parents worked on the land – and they had to tip their hats to the farmer because he owned the land where they lived so he owned them basically ... my parents grew up that way and so I took on the personality of someone who was oppressed I couldn't go to University, I was a land worker, a labourer, that's all you can do, that is what I was taught – a psychological oppression I suppose' (8Y1J).

'We're all puppets aren't we? I don't want to be a puppet any more. I've been enlightened and I don't want to be oppressed ... oppression is important, because once you're enlightened you don't

want to be shackled, you want to be free ... I think this is something else the course teaches you is to think for yourself, rather than have society think for you as a collective thought ... I do like that about the course' (15Y2W).

'Oppression is a very hard word. I'm not 100% sure of the definition of oppression, but the way I see it is Oppression is like a down force, that's how I see it, which makes me think obviously that people at the top are trying to step on the people below' (17Y2C).

Equality

'A wonderful concept, but the over-riding question for me is as one of my fellow teacher's said, who do I want to be equal with?' (1TTJ).

'I believe that every single person should be equal ... I also think we should regard many other life forms as equal as well ... Unfortunately they are not; they have been dragged down to the level of commodities, as most people are. I truly believe that everybody is equal but not say, for example, intellectually, I believe that everybody has certain skills that make them equal and just as valuable, as everybody else' (2TTS).

'For meeveryone in the class is very much on an equal basis and nobody should stamp all over peoples viewpoints ... there is still the

178

equality of opportunity for people to discuss things ... it's very different from being in a class of say sixteen students, where you are all debating questions backwards and forwards and the tutor is involved, compared to being in a lecture hall with two hundred students and just going through power point slides ... where there is very little interaction at all ... I pass on knowledge so that we can all be equally involved in the group progress and development' (3TTV).

'Since doing this Degree my mind's been completely opened up ... it has completely opened up my mind into a different way of thinking to what the world is really about' (17Y2C).

'It doesn't matter if you are disabled, or what colour you are, or if you can't put a sentence together, or whether you are a social phobic, everybody has something to give' (25PSS).

Freedom

'Realistically no one can ever have total freedom from our physical and psychological needs until the point of death, which I suppose is behind the saying 'rest in peace'' (1TTJ).

'You can be free in any system as long as your mind is free but you have to deprogram and deconstruct all of the societal programming you have had throughout your life ... we are already filled up with

179

society, so you have to break that down again ... everything that has socialised you has made you part of the system, so you have to start internally deconstructing it before you can even begin to experience the concept of freedom' (2TTS).

'I felt I was trapped in a system that I couldn't change and that did make me feel sad. It did make me feel a little bit helpless, but I also think knowledge is freedom, because once you identify something you can work within a system ... the freedom to think, the freedom to learn' (5TTD).

'Freedom ... is it in education? Is it in the outside world? I think it's just the most fundamental thing that you could have as a human really ... I think it's something a lot of people don't have. I think it's probably something that most people want to obtain at some point. It's something that people dream of' (11Y1S).

'I've learnt more from the free way these teachers taught me, than I did in the entire time in my secondary school' (18Y3C).

Transformation

'I have definitely been transformed by education, as well as my life experiences…What started me wanting to do my doctorate was seeing how my students said they had been transformed by doing the Degree and I have seen it in myself too' (1TTJ).

'I would say definitely in further education, definitely at Degree level … I hope I am part of an ongoing and growing movement of people who are waking up and realising what is going on … I feel the world needs more action and more people to realise what is going on because no system can last forever and capitalism is a system the same as anything else … We were encouraged to be critical thinkers and in all my lectures I encourage a set of questioning and breaking down ideas' (2TTS).

'Transformation, human beings need to grow and evolve and I grew and evolved through what I did on the Degree and I am helping other people to do that. I think we all need to have our eyes opened. I think education is fantastic for transformation in a way, in the formal setting, cause it certainly happened to me, but also there are informal settings as well that you can enable that to happen' (5TTD).

'Transformation is what I am doing here … a transformation from my old way of life' (8Y1J).

'Transformation-I think that's what education especially can do for you. It's changed me so much. I'm still struggling with it … at first it made me really nervous and I was on the edge a bit, but I feel it's a place of belonging … It makes me feel that I'm doing something with my life' (11Y1S).

'I'd say I haven't transformed completely, but I'm transforming. I don't think the transition is completely done yet … I'm still questioning everything' (17Y2C).

Enlightenment

'My enlightenment has been mainly about education… enlightenment is about life experiences and definitely about education' (1TTJ).

'I feel that education should be about enlightening people and waking them up from their mass media induced coma … You have got to have some sort of critical thinking. I permanently instil in my

students that it is only by asking difficult questions and by being a critical thinker that society progresses' (2TTS).

'Enlightenment for me is probably the most important thing in education because it's a sense of knowing that there are broader things out there than just the humdrum things in life ... The world just isn't about how much money can we make, it's about enlightening your spirit, your soul ... becoming more of a person and looking at the world through different eyes ... and when you can see it, there's a spark in student's, you can see them start to challenge ideas and become a bit more enlightened to alternative view points. That for me is one of the best parts of the job' (3TTV).

'Enlightenment ... To me that says being made aware, which I feel how this course has enlightened me to life ... someone turning the light on ... and you try to spread that to other people ... it certainly feels like an enlightenment, definitely' (15Y2W).

'I think with enlightenment when you can open your mind to anything out there that anything is possible then all of these other things 'transformation, freedom, equality, oppression and democracy' can all come under 'enlightenment'. So I think that you realise what all these things are about. Without enlightenment I *don't think that you can really fully have the capacity to realise what the other things are about' (19Y3T).*

'Enlightenment is the exact same thing as transformation some people can do this Degree and they are still going to have their one-sided opinions' (18Y3C).

Summary, Interview Question 5

- Democracy – On average this concept was not given too much credence. Some participants felt it did not and could never exist in reality – it was thought of more as an ideal for society to aspire to

- Oppression – This prompt raised the question as to what this terminology actually meant to each participant. Responses ranged from oppression of the mind to oppressive regimes in the classroom, capitalism and gender roles

- Equality – This prompt gained similar responses to Democracy in that it was considered to be an ideal but not necessarily realistic. The overall response seemed to relate to one particular member of the Teaching Team stance *'who do you want to be equal with'?*

- Freedom – The responses overall reflected members of the Teaching Team viewpoints in that participants did not refer to this concept much in terms of a physical form of restraint, but related it more to a freedom of the mind. Several references were made to education as a medium for achieving freedom of the mind as opposed to capitalism as a restraint upon this type of freedom and expression

- Transformation – This prompt was again referred to in terms of educational experiences and teaching practices, particularly relating to the confidence and ability to question their teachers and peers openly. All of the participants in the research felt they had been 'transformed' mainly in terms of increased awareness of societal inequalities and the confidence to communicate effectively with each other

- Enlightenment – Similar to the prompt Transformation the viewpoints expressed by the participants related to education and an increased awareness, as a sense of knowing

Interview Question 6; can you tell me how the experiences of being a student in your classes has effected how you see yourself as a student, in terms of your role and Student Identity?

This question involved asking the current and previous student participants about the possible affects the course and teaching practices had upon them in terms of their role and personal identity. As transformative teaching practices are associated with personal change and subsequent agency the question was asked to explore whether their responses reflected the findings from the review of literature.

Responses given by the current/previous students

'It is liberating because it opens up new possibilities. I was going to be a land worker until I retired – like my Father ... I have never done anything academic - my Father got me a job through a friend when I left school- that was it – that was my career path as it were ... Then I went from one job to another – as I say I worked continually for 25 years' (8Y1J).

'I was just the cook, cleaner, bottle-washer and that sort of thing before. Now I'm more of an inspiration ... and I feel a sense of achievement ... it's all very positive ... other than the late nights and

186

the lack of sleep cause you're bouncing ideas off somebody else, cause even though there wasn't much sleep you come in the next day and it's all still quite fresh ... that sort of thing helps a lot' (15Y2W).

'When I am here I'm a student and when I'm at home, I'm a parent but I think I see myself as becoming a person in my own right, whereas before it was almost like I was drifting and I didn't think about how I felt inside or where I was going to go, but now I do ... I actually love being here, I love being in college ... you can give so much more through education ...My knowledge, I suppose ... What I've gained out of it; I would like to pass onto somebody else ... Give somebody else that enlightenment. That's what I would like ... Definitely' (19Y3T).

'I see myself getting on that PGCE course, getting in school ... teaching instead of being taught ... I can see me passing on everything I've learnt ... I just love the subject, I love it ...I do love it. You have got yourselves to thank for that though ... you have given the tools ... and now it's however you use it isn't it?' (23PSR).

Summary, Interview Question 6

- Clearly for the first year student (8Y1J) emphasis has been given to a change from a traditional manual labouring role to that of an academic student identity which he found liberating and likely to lead to a different career path

- For the female student(15Y2W) more emphasis was given to her role as a student and part of a group helping each other to revise and learn. There is also a clear gender difference associated with traditional working class roles and identity compared to that of the male student (8Y1J). For the female this sense of identity and role in life was related to house work and to the male, manual labour

- Issues of class and gender roles were raised several times throughout the interviews in terms of educational experiences and teaching practice. The participant responses generated from Question 6 and throughout the entire interviews will be subjected to an in depth analysis in Chapter Five with reference to class and gender issues

- The third year female participants' (19Y3T) response also reflects gender issues in that her sense of identity was very much about being a parent. This participant considered that as a result of her educational experiences she would like to pass on her newly gained sense of enlightenment, demonstrating an increased sense of agency and change concerning her role in life and identity

- The previous student (23PSR) wished to pass 'on everything I've learnt' because she had been given the 'tools' to do so from her teachers on the course. This student's response also demonstrates a change in her personal agency as she now wishes to become a teacher herself

- These current and previous student responses demonstrated that their transformational teaching experiences and the 'tools' they had been given engendered an increased sense of agency and a desire to teach in the same tranformatory style they themselves have experienced

Interview Question 6TP; can you tell me how the experiences of being a student in these classes have affected your Teaching Practice?'

All of the questions for the teaching team participants throughout the interviews were identical to those asked of the current and previous student participants with the exception of the last question

(Q6) which was replaced by Q6TP (Coded for Teaching Practice). Following a review of the literature and with consideration of my own positionality, I explored whether my former students who are now teachers had been affected by the teaching experiences they had received on the course.

The teacher's responses confirmed this was the case, as my knowledge and observation of the Teaching Team members had previously indicated, the tranformatory teaching practice had been reproduced, and as a result our quest to instil a sense of agency and enlightenment in individuals had been achieved. In this sense the previous, current, and future students developed a desire for addressing the inequalities within society, for female, working class individuals in particular. The following quotes from the teachers, beginning with my own, illustrate the responses gained from Question 6TP.

'Doing the O.U. Degree, as a student was great in that I had all the resources necessary laid out for me ... but it was such a lonely and confusing experience. I found it really distressing, not to be able to ask someone even about the simplest things because I felt too ashamed to say that I didn't understand something ... I also felt that

because I hadn't been able to understand the academic terminology on the tape I must be a bit 'thick'... I now realise this is how my students might feel if they haven't got any one to talk to. So my teaching practice always involves class discussions and giving the students the confidence to be able to ask anything they want without feeling 'thick'. So for me my life experiences and my academic journey are definitely reflected in my teaching practices' (1TTJ).

'As a Degree student I found it very enlightening and uplifting and I learned to question more... so in my classes everybody gets the chance to speak, so I would say that instead of actually teaching I am just a discussion organiser ... I don't actually teach as such, I throw out ideas and then let people discuss them and think about them...I like to have an open forum where everybody gets to say something and I encourage people who are naturally quiet to talk more than the ones who are naturally loud'(2TTS).

'I struggled with sociology as you well know. But I think with the encouragement and always being told that you, and your opinion was just as valid as the person who was getting firsts when you were getting 40%, were still just as valid ... I changed through my Degree from the encouragement from the teachers feedback, support, and

feeling part of it. This is what I now do to my students ... because I'm so approachable ... they are comfortable with me and if they are comfortable they're more likely to learn and challenge you ... that's what I learnt on my studies and that's what I try and give to my student's(4TTJS).

'We were in small groups ... discussing, with peers and then the tutor was going round and talking to each group and chatting with them ... in close proximity to you and then actually challenge you directly to go and research something. So I challenge mine ... it's how I teach, because it had an impact on me and I realised that is how I want my students to learn because some of the things that I teach in Sociology are challenging ... we were challenged, but we had support. We had someone there we could go to and say 'help, help - I don't understand this, or what do I do?' So I want them to be able to come to me and I do have a very good relationship with my students ... they can come to me that's how I learnt and it was good for me' (5TTD).

Summary, Interview Question 6TP

- *The account I gave as an Open University student was in complete contrast to the transformative teaching I received*

192

as an Undergraduate at a HE College. At College I was
able to talk to my peers and teachers instead of studying
from a book in isolation and we were also encouraged to
question everything we had been told was established
'facts' in society. As a result of these teaching practices I
gained an enlightenment and awareness of inequalities in
society and a desire to teach in the same way I had been
taught there (1TTJ)

- The member of the Teaching Team (2TTS) who states that he likes to have an 'open forum' rather than actually teach clearly reflects the critical thinking style of teaching. In addition the comments made about ensuring that all the people have the chance to speak reflects the work of feminist writers such as bell hooks (1994), as the more mature females tend to be the quieter students until they build up the confidence to speak up for themselves. Throughout virtually all of the interviews participants refer to their increase in confidence as a result of working in small groups and being given the opportunity to gain a 'voice'

- The teacher who talked about being 'approachable' (4TTJS)provides a clear demonstration as to how the 'familiarity of teachers' (coded as DFT) can have an effect upon teaching practices, particularly in an FE environment rather than that of a large University. As this teacher points out if a student feels 'comfortable' with their teacher and teaching practices on their course, they will be *'feeling part of it'* and a member of a community of learners (hooks, 1994)

- Dana (5TTD)reflects the statement made by Jess(4TTJS)in that the teaching practices at the Riverside East College are challenging but also very supportive. Obviously the environment and the smaller number of students at an FE College provides more opportunities for the teachers to work on a one to one basis more frequently than in a University where many more students are taught in lecture halls rather than in small discussion groups

- The link between how the teachers were taught at the Riverside East College and how it affects their own teaching was clearly established

Additional Research Findings, Metaphors used in the Research Interviews

Initially the use of metaphors in the research design was not given a great deal of importance although having taught psychoanalysis theory and the associated methodology for several years I was aware of how individuals often use them liberally in an attempt to describe their conscious or unconscious thoughts and feelings. After discussing teaching and learning experiences both past and present with the participants during the research interviews I soon became aware as to the extent they had been used both by myself and the other participants. As a result I went back to my review of literature and read extensively upon the credence given as both a methodology in itself and as a form of analysis within qualitative research. Schmitt (2005, p.358) supports the emphasis now given to the use of metaphors within the study of cognitive linguistics and states:

'For almost all qualitative methods of research, language is at one and the same time subject and medium. It is used above all as material referring to content outside language: patterns of relationships, latent structures of meaning, communicative strategies, etc.'

As this research was literally all about teaching practices involving discussions and communication I began to realise just how important the use of metaphors was within my own qualitative research. The participants used several metaphors to encapsulate their thoughts and feelings during their interviews. On several occasions the metaphor 'my eyes were opened' was used to describe the transformational effects they had experienced as a result of teaching practices received upon the Degree. Selections of the metaphors are included within this chapter in order to provide a sound basis for the analysis of the research findings in the following chapter. Within the following Chapter Five references are made as to how hooks (1994), Schmitt, (2005) considered that metaphors can provide an in depth, conscious and unconscious enlightenment to this type of terminology and discourse.

Examples of Metaphors used within the Interviews

'At school I felt that I was a round peg in a square hole' (1TTJ).

The use of this metaphor encapsulates the feelings I had as a child from a working class family who gained a scholarship to study in a very posh all girls Grammar School. I just did not feel I belonged because of my home environment and the working class culture associated with it.

'I give them the basic building blocks and I expect them to come back and have built me a palace' (2TTS).

Saul explained that he wanted the Undergraduates to '*go out there to explore for themselves'.* This response and use of metaphors demonstrates that as a teacher Saul was clearly encouraging the development and sense of agency in the students.

'The books we used were always Jeff Petty- rather like painting by numbers – only this was teaching by numbers'(3TTV).

When speaking about one of his previous educational experiences (teacher training) Vincent considered he was taught that teaching should be about following procedures in a formulaic fashion, with little or no encouragement for the students to reflect or question what the teacher said. The use of metaphors within this response seems to demonstrate that Vincent did not wish to teach in the same style he had been taught on a teaching course, which provides

197

support for the data gained from Question 6TP (teaching practices). Clearly, the manner in which Vincent was taught on the Degree Course, which encouraged critical thinking, is the complete opposite of the *'teaching by numbers'* experience he received when undertaking the teacher training course, indicating that he was fully aware of the effect the different styles had upon learners.

'There is a point where you have been quite happy in your little bubble of ignorance ... then you learn about Marxism and you can't stay in your little bubble ... it lit my fire...massive eye opener... Epiphany - definitely one of the main things I took away from the Degree' (5TTD).

Dana explained that after being challenged to defend her previously held beliefs during her Undergraduate studies, and with particular regard to her comment, *'you learn about Marxism'* she became more aware of the inequality and oppression in society and as a result she adopted a more cynical, political view of the world. The use of the metaphors *'massive eye opener... Epiphany'* indicates that she had gained a sense of awareness and enlightenment from the research course teaching experiences. The use of the metaphor *'happy in your little bubble of ignorance'* also indicates that there can be a sense of fear associated with this newly gained sense of awareness and escape from being in a state of 'ignorance' (Fromm, 1961, Freire and Shor, 1986, hooks, 1994).

'It's liberating – I have thrown off the old shackles – it's kind of like a caterpillar turning into a butterfly'(8Y1J).

As the Riverside East College is set within a rural socio-economically deprived area many of the Undergraduates are brought up to have few, if any educational aspirations. To break free from these working class traditional values (reference to *'the old shackles'?)* is clearly a liberating although sometimes quite a frightening experience for them, or as Jack also stated *'it is out of my comfort zone by a very long way'* (Fromm, 1961, Freire and Shor, 1986, hooks, 1994). The metaphor of changing from a *'caterpillar turning into a butterfly'* also suggests that a sense of freedom and liberation has been gained as a result of the Research Course educational experiences.

'I didn't feel I was very naïve, but I must have been, bobbing along in my own little world, until I think probably Saul started it, made me think about everything, realised that the world wasn't quite as I'd

seen it and I didn't like him for that for a little while, cause he did burst my bubble and I was a little bit upset about that'(14Y2A).

This current student seems to be echoing the previous ones in that she talks metaphorically about being in her own *'little world' in a 'bubble'* which can, for some be quite a comforting place until it is 'burst' by a critical and questioning educational experience. This Undergraduate also seems to suggest that by questioning, rather than that of a previous state of acceptance, can result in a new sense of awareness from the bursting of the 'bubble'. Angela states that previously she was *'just accepting things ... Whatever you were told, that was it, there was nothing else, you couldn't think about it yourself ... you didn't question adult's because they knew everything and you just kind of did as you were told and you were quiet in the corner ... now I can think for myself, which is actually really nice'.*

The metaphor of being *'quiet in the corner'* also represents several of the female students in particular in that they found a 'voice' as a result of being given opportunities to speak out and discuss their opinions within the safety of their learning community (hooks, 1994).

'I felt, before I started this, that I'd been asleep' (17Y2C).

Cathy talked about how prior to studying on the Degree she was permanently 'asleep' and then described how '*it has completely opened up my mind into a different way of thinking to what the world is really about, because when I grew up it was have an education or go to work. You've got to live somehow*'. Surprisingly perhaps, no mention of 'the world' was made within the interview questions, and yet it was used repeatedly throughout the narratives, and responses, indicating that as Freire, (1996, p.62) states 'Education as the practice of freedom - as opposed to education as the practice of domination - denies that man is abstract, isolated, independent, and unattached to the world; it also denies that the world exists as a reality apart from people', as previously quoted in the introduction of this research.

'If I had not done this Degree I would still be one-sided and I would still be like a machine in a system' (18Y3C).

Carlos a young male student uses the metaphor of being part of a machine as an employee (an inference previously made to capitalism) that '*has been designed to benefit, what I feel are the top 1% rather than the 99% ... I now know one benefit of just pure knowledge is it allows me the tools...even if I only help 50 people, it is still going to do more for me than if I stayed in that machine'.* Carlos clearly considered that education is 'the tool' that can be used to break free from capitalist power structures or as he metaphorically states '*a machine in a system'*.

'Children who are having problems fitting into main stream schools who aren't able to follow the curriculum as they are expected to because it is almost like a 'one size fits all' (19Y3T).

Tina expressed her concerns about children having to '*follow by rote in a way that they have to learn it in a certain manner ... this is what is expected of children ... I realise that in schools they have a certain amount of people and they have to follow the rules, they have to do it in a certain way. But here in our Degree we still manage with 25 people in the group to have a conversation. We are all maintaining our own identities and we are still learning, where in schools I don't feel that is the case'.* It would seem that by using the '*one size fits all'* metaphor Tina associates a lack of communication with a loss of an individual's identity and ability to learn. It would also seem that she is making a link between the marketisation of education and the teaching of children, almost like a factory making clothes.

'I try and put myself in that person's shoes ... I try to put myself to think out of the box'(21Y3S).

Sally discussed in her interview how she approached her essay work and how she felt that it was necessary to not just cover the theories and literature it had to be more than that, she had to relate her work to real individuals living within a real world. In order to stay within the remits of her assignment requirements however Sally felt that by *'discussing ideas with other people in the group it does help because they can tell me if they think I'm going off on a tangent, and speaking to you now, well you know, I speak to all you lecturers'*

'I used to have quite a black and white sort of way of thinking, but I've started to realise now more with this course that life isn't like that. It's not that clear cut, it's not black and white, and there are loads of grey areas' (22Y3A).

Anita stated that her 'way of thinking' has been transformed from 'black and white' to 'grey' since she began her studies on this course. Furthermore she now wishes to teach herself and encourage her own future students to think in a more 'open' manner which clearly reflects a rejection of the banking system of teaching practices *'I think that's one big thing that I've learnt and I would*

203

like to teach my students to be open minded, make their own decisions, make their own choices, encourage them to go as far as they can'

'God, look how they've come on in the last year. Unbelievable, the leaps that some people make' (23PSR).

Roxy was particularly keen to talk about how the course enabled her and her peers to find a voice and as such she felt she changed as a result of being given the opportunity to speak and contribute to class discussions. *'I think we all become opinionated. We did, I think even the ones who started off really quiet at the back of the classroom found their voice by the end of the course. I do think that. When you look at people who probably would never have dreamed that they would pass a Degree and you see them, and they come on…loads, loads, loads of people, everybody changed on the course in a positive way everyone did'.*

'Sometimes it might be quite nice to go back into your bubble but you cannot go back into your bubble, so you have to take a responsibility for the fact that you do know that, and that is quite a big responsibility to have'(27PSJ).

Joan (27PSJ) used the same metaphor as Dana *(5TTD)* that of living in a 'bubble' which they both thought can be quite a comfortable place to be prior to studying sociology on the Degree and gaining a sense of awareness and a different kind of knowledge regarding the world and society. This new sense of awareness can however be quite a challenge in that Joan also states, *'It is powerful, but also lonely, and I think perhaps that is something else that doing a Degree, -perhaps knowledge, - you cannot undo knowledge you have learnt.'* Joan is also teaching now at the Riverside East College and like Dana, talks about how this escape from the bubble engendered an overwhelming desire to pass on this new sense of awareness and knowledge to their own Undergraduate students. The desire to become an agent of change and awareness was she felt, now her responsibility as a Teacher of Social History at the Riverside East College.

Initial Summary of the Findings

The overall findings from the interview questions and narratives reported in this chapter informed the analysis of the participants' responses as reported in the next Chapter Five. The rich and valid data generated from the interview questions reported in this chapter also justified and validated the methodology to demonstrate the transformational effects the critical teaching experienced had upon the participants. In particular the progression from the Stages one, two and three was demonstrated Freire, 1996, Sweet, (1989).

Descriptive factors gained from the cycle 1 exercise were formulated in order to produce the Tables in the Appendix Section and the narrative summaries of each question in this Chapter Four. This process proved to be similar to a treasure hunt, looking for the most appropriate jewels of information from the mountains of rubies, diamonds and emeralds, such was the quality of the humanised data gained from the quotes, and the review of literature in Chapter Two. Again, the main problem that arose was what to leave out from the enormous saturation of highly appropriate and valid data generated from the interview questions.

So please join me now to see how in Chapter Five a response to the Research Questions and the Review of Literature (Chapter Two) was produced. The research design as demonstrated in the Methodology (Chapter Three) is also reviewed with consideration as to the validity of sampling procedures, and the subjective interpretation of the participant responses. An additional analysis of the section associated with the interpretation of Metaphors is also recorded in Chapter Five which I found particularly enjoyable to report upon.

Chapter Five Thematic Data Analysis

Introduction

In this chapter a thematic analysis of the findings demonstrates and connects the participants overall responses and quotes gained from each of the six questions, with the review of the literature. The consolidation of the responses and the review of literature form an analysis and thematic coverage of the Research Questions. Some of the themes were consolidated and other things arose, which had not been previously considered, such as the analysis of the metaphors used in the review of literature, and the participants' responses.

The Research Questions were developed in association with my positionality and life experiences, both as a student and a teacher, and the review of literature (Chapter Two). The Research Questions were also developed as an effective and appropriate qualitative methodology in order to explore the main aims of the research. It was considered appropriate to reflect upon these considerations as a reflexive example of praxis. As I am attempting to be guided by and follow Freire's work, I need to continually reflect upon my own actions and transformational experiences, in terms of my own praxis. This is a particularly appropriate factor with regard to Research Question 3, in order to explore whether I had gained more of a sense of empowerment and agency as a result of researching my own teaching practice and experiences of transformational teaching. Within this chapter, emphasis is given to addressing the issues associated with the Research Questions in more depth. The summarised research findings demonstrated below are also thematically and explicitly linked to the Review of Literature sub headings used in Chapter Two.

The Process and Development of the Review of Literature

It became apparent from the review of literature and the teachers who have been providing transformational educational experiences, that people can be literally transformed and changed as a result of their interactions with their peers and teachers. In particular the transformational teaching practices studied at the Riverside East College provided clear evidence as to the extent previous interactions between the teacher and the learner can instil a new sense of personal identity and engender a change to their own version of reality.

The Teaching Environment and the Learning Landscape

Carol (7TTC) considered that as a result of the teaching 'techniques' used at the Riverside East College she now felt that she could *'interact with what is going on...you don't have to just sit there watching the news passively ... you become a participant in it and allowed to discuss it ... whereas I wouldn't believe I had anything to add ... and that is from the teaching ... it set you free'.* Carol's response can be thought of as supporting the Research Questions 1 and 2 with regard to the teaching practices upon the research course promoting feelings of agency and empowerment, and the restriction of such from her prior educational experiences at school and within the home environment.

During the narrative interviews it also became apparent that the females in particular considered their prior educational experiences were a secondary issue compared to the need to make money. Anita (19Y3A) stated that *'I couldn't wait to leave school; I couldn't get out of school quick enough. I just wanted to go out and earn money'.* Anita's comments were reflected in those made by Angela (14Y2A) *'I didn't enjoy primary or secondary education ... a lot of people were there to make friends but I just wanted to get out of school and make money.'*

The need to make money rather than gain educational experiences as a female adult was explicitly linked to Joan's (27PSJ) comments who narrated that *'nobody that I went to school with went to University, even those that were in the top stream went into apprenticeship ... I went for the first job that was available as a*

Junior Accountancy Apprentice at £40 per week ... and because it was such bad pay, I worked Saturdays and Sundays as a waitress as well'. The comments made by the majority of females regarding employment, class issues and role expectations were also supported by the male participant Jack (8Y1J) who stated that *'In my time when I was young you left school and got a job. They all worked on the land ... you had to do what your father did and what your grandfather did.'*

Political Effects upon the Learning Environment

The political implications of teaching in a transformational style were substantially supported within the Research conclusions. As Neary (2012, p.149) explains 'the public sphere is identified as the way in which political power is organised across society. This organisation of political power is referred to as the state'. The Research participants repeatedly referred to how they were subjected to this type of political power within school in particular, by being subjected to the banking style of teaching which merely reproduced traditional historical facts in order to maintain the 'status quo' of the state and capitalist influences.

Interestingly, with regard to my own Undergraduate studies between 1989 until 1992 my student grant was a life line and provided me with more financial security than I had ever had, and although I had some of the student loan to pay back it was a very small debt compared to what the current students are amounting now. This particular time period is cited within Canaan's et al. (2011, p.5) research as being significant in that 'University used to be a class barrier in itself; it now reflects, within student bodies (at 'pre-and post 92 institutions) the various gradations of our class system' Little (2010, p.12). Judging from the participants responses regarding employment and financial reasons, even if like Canaan et al. students it is not explicitly referred to in those terms, class consciousness was a highly important factor associated with their transformational educational experiences.

Another salient issue arises with respect to the question of class in this respect is that of contextualisation, for me as a working class female, a Student Grant was a motivational factor to going to University in that it provided me with a stable income in the 1980's, and paid my fees. With the introduction of Student Loans and the huge increase in Student fees in 2014 this may have become a crucial factor for many potential University students in deciding whether to undertake this form of study or not. The type of subjects students opt to study could also be linked to potential career opportunities in order to pay the loans back, as discussed in the introduction of this research, and the work of Amsler regarding the marketisation of education and neoliberalism within the Review of Literature (Chapter Two).

The Production and Marketisation of knowledge

Within the review of the literature (Chapter two) attention was given to how higher education could be thought of as a 'public good' (Stuart, 2012, Amsler 2010, 2011, 2013). According to Stuart (2012, p.1) therefore it is necessary to challenge 'the marketisation and commodification of higher education and ask how far is it possible to promote equality through higher education by using extended and open access, student choice and the scholarship of teaching and learning.' Certainly within this Research it was concluded that the participants had been subjected to the marketisation of learning by having a substantial increase in their student fees, and across the UK there has been a reduction in Undergraduate courses that encourage critical thought, which is generated by transformational teaching (Amsler 2010, 2011, 2013).

Furthermore Neary (2012, p.149) proposes that 'The private sphere relates primarily to the ways in which everyday social life is dominated by marketised and commercial activities that are organised and regulated across society as part of a generalised economic system'. From the Research findings it was concluded that the participants' prior experiences of being taught in the banking style of teaching did have an oppressive influence upon their everyday lives by denying them the opportunities to challenge the capitalist 'status quo' dictates.

At the Riverside East College, as with just about every University in the UK, Undergraduate courses have to reveal the 'employability factors' associated with the educational experience within their promotional prospectus now. As the discipline of sociology itself challenges the power structures within society often associated with employment factors within a neoliberalist, and capitalist society, this dictate does, to a certain extent prevent, or at the very least minimises my own empowerment and agency within the classroom (Research Question 3).

The Production and the Control of Knowledge

Within my transformational and critical teaching practice I often discuss with the Undergraduates essay questions, and whenever possible offer them the choice of producing their own assessment questions, although this obviously has to be agreed with the University Module Leaders, and fall within the dictated University 'Learning outcomes'. With consideration to these dictates these aspects fall under the umbrella of the Research Question 3 with regard to my own transformational teaching practices and to my own empowerment within the classroom, and by contrast the prevention of my own agency in the external context of the dictated University 'Learning outcomes'.

Judging from the responses given to Interview Question 2 in particular, (how teaching practices impacted upon you)Vincent (3TTV) had clearly become aware of the perils continuing to believe the 'facts' that had been installed into him as a child experiencing the banking system (Freire, 1996) used in teaching practices at his school. By contrast when considering the impact of the teaching practices used at the Riverside East College Vincent responded that there is a *'need to question everything, because what may be apparent today and is gospel in terms of theory and research may be obsolete in ten years' time ... so yeah it definitely had an effect upon me ... and how I relate to others as well, it can make you quite argumentative, but also sensitive to others needs'*

Oppressive Power Structures, Class and Gender issues

Issues of class and gender was demonstrated as being responsible for some of the participants feeling they had been oppressed, although obviously this is not the case for every female or male, or every working class person. As this research was about transformational forms of teaching sociology in particular I explored how this can lead to empowerment and agency and reflect the work of Gerke (2013, p.1) who considers that:

> 'A number of sociologists understand their work as being part of a radical or transformative project. They are committed to empowering the marginalised or are engaged in challenging hegemony ... and understand their work as a contribution to laying foundations for a more just, equal and democratic society'.

For the female participants in particular a correlation became apparent between the teaching practices they had experienced at school and their traditionally held beliefs of societal issues such as class and gender. As a result almost all of the female participants reported that as they gained confidence to ask questions and discuss societal issues at the Riverside East College they had gained an increased level of awareness of these issues and a huge difference in their levels of self-confidence.

With regard to class issues, not many of the participants spoke of this as directly being a key factor within the process of their personal transformation. I was surprised by this apparent lack of recognition within the narratives especially as their sociological studies are directly related to class issues. I was however pleased that my research findings reflected those of Canaan, Jenkins, Filippakou and Strudwick (2011) who also found that from their sociology student's autobiographies class did not seem to register significantly in their participants responses.

In this respect Canaan et al. (2011, p.05) wanted to explore what seemed to be a pedagogical 'failure' to instil the importance of class issues within their sociology students concerning their identities and life chances. These authors found it particularly troublesome that within society and sociological research, class issues were often considered to be 'so confusing and complicated … as to be analytically useless' (Harvey, 2010, p.232). The research conducted by Canaan et al. (2011) was also particularly relevant to understanding and analysing my research findings as their students were from working class backgrounds, who like mine were 'often the first generation in their families to attend University and with parents having jobs such as factory workers and low level support or service workers' Canaan et al. (2011, p.6). Apart from one student all of the participants were from working class backgrounds for whom educational and employment experiences were dominated by financial necessities.

Carol (7TTC) was one of the only participants to mention class issues when discussing how she felt that the teaching practices at the Riverside East College had set her 'free'. Carol remarked *'I am not harping on about class, but my class generation was taught you do as you are told and there's an input, output expectation – you are going to stack shelves at Woolworth's … it's not for you to make those sorts of decisions … that's above your station.'*

Within the narratives associated with Interview Question 1 in particular, (experience of education since leaving school) virtually all of the female participants stated that they had thought differently about how they might have been oppressed either at school, by their families or adult relationships. During the teaching experiences at the Riverside East College I become aware that for several females increased levels of awareness and of self-confidence had an effect upon their marital status, which again can be viewed by the individuals concerned from both a positive or negative angle. Judging from the narratives none of the males reported that an increased level of confidence had affected their marital status, whereas for the females this did seem to be a considerable factor. During the narrative responses the female Jess (4TTJS) reported that *'you learn to stand up for yourself with a decent argument and therefore my marriage ended at the beginning of the second year, with my husband saying the worst thing I ever did was come to college.'*

Dana (5TTD) who also experienced the end of her 18 year marriage during her period of studies stated in her narrative that *'I really grew as a person between the beginning of the Access and the end of the Degree. I was a changed person. Sometimes it is a painful process and it did have effects on some parts of my personal life – but no regrets because sometimes I think a little bit of pain are needed to get through- to a certain point.'* The notion of pain that Dana talked of can be thought of in negative terms, as a fear of freedom can be (Fromm, 1961), but again her response indicates that in order to *'get through'* it can also be thought of as yielding a positive outcome.

Although my research is not about how teaching practices can have an effect upon marital status, it is about how participants can become more enlightened concerning injustices within their personal life and society, and as a result of a transformational teaching practice become more motivated to engender change through personal agency.

Although obviously it would be impossible to conclude that all personal relationships had either changed or ended as a direct result of increased awareness of 'previously inconspicuous phenomena' thematically the narrative responses indicated there could be a relationship between the two. Furthermore, as well as the increased levels of awareness of oppressive practices within relationships, and an increase in their personal confidence, all of the female participants reported they felt more able to become active agents and as such instigate change in this direction if desired or considered necessary.

Critical Thinking, a means of Escape from Oppression

From the participants' responses, including those from the teaching team, it could be seen that the individuals had to first become aware of their former oppression as a result of educational practices, before they could achieve a sense of freedom and thus become reborn and experience 'humanisation.' As a participant (1TTJ) I commented upon how I became aware of my own oppression when responding to Question 5 regarding the themes that emerged from my educational experiences by stating that '*As an adult, I now realise that oppression can be something that is not only about physical elements, but more importantly perhaps it is about the oppression of mind as well*'.

It became apparent that the participants experienced 'Education as the practice of freedom –as opposed to education as the practice of domination' Freire (1996, p.27). Virtually all of the participants considered their previous educational experiences, particularly at school, as characterised by a practice of domination, whereas the teaching practices at the Riverside East College offered them a sense of freedom to question their traditionally held beliefs of political and social inequalities.

It would seem from the participants' responses that growing up in a local, rural and economically socially deprived environment indicated that this was a factor in the maintenance of traditionally held beliefs often associated with working class gender roles. During their studies at the Riverside East College these traditional viewpoints were challenged within their gender studies. As a result many of the female participants made similar comments such as Roxy's (23PSR) regarding her return to studies as an adult at the Riverside East College in that there was a growing realisation that '*I am capable of doing it and so you come back, - I feel it is cathartic*'.

As a result of the teaching practices in which they were encouraged to speak out and discuss gender issues at the Riverside East College, most of the participants had become more aware of the extent they had been oppressed within their adult relationships. In this respect Freire, (1996, p.63) points out 'As women and men, simultaneously reflecting on themselves and on the world, increase the scope of their perception, they begin to direct their observations towards previously inconspicuous phenomena'.

The Question of 'Reality' and Dominating Ideologies

The Research findings clearly demonstrated that the participants own versions of reality, with particular regard to class and gender positions within society, have been effectively addressed throughout this research, and explicitly linked to the authors referred to within the review of literature. A correlation between all of the participants' positionality, and the relevance of teaching practices has been established with consideration to each person's versions of reality.

With regard to the teaching practices, and dominating ideologies, the participants reported that theywere not encouraged to even consider further education, and as Carol (7TTC) stated they should 'know their place'. As Freire (1996) considered that this type of teaching experiences were responsible for not only instilling a culture of silence, but also for ensuring that this status was maintained, it is somewhat ironic that the participants often spoke of how they did not have the confidence to speak out under these conditions.

By contrast, and in accordance with Freire, (1996), Neary, (2011, 2012), Amsler et al. (2010), Allman, (2010), when individuals gained a state of critical awareness of dominating ideologies and oppressive practices in both the public and private sector, they also experienced enhanced levels of political awareness. Again, ironically when reporting the impact of latter transformational styles of teaching they experienced, the participants stated they had gained enhanced levels of self-confidence, and as such gained a voice and overcome this 'culture of silence'.

Teaching Practices, the Banking Concept of Education, Effects upon Students.

For all but one of the female participants their experiences of school and teaching practices inhibited creativity. Carol (7TTC) summarised the negative interactions between teachers and girls in particular by stating that '*I think that at school you were very much trained to work in Woolworths, it never really occurred to them that we were going to do anything else, so we weren't encouraged to think creatively or to take ownership of our learning'.* The teacher expectations and relationship with the schoolgirls was also summarised by Joan (27PSJ) who remarked that *'there was absolutely no encouragement for aspiration, so I was given a very stark choice that I could become a typist… or a hairdresser'.*

Several of the participants speaking about the prior teaching styles they had encountered at school, or on behalf of their own children, considered that the teaching practices at school had the effect of being 'primed' for society by making them conform to dictated societal standards and values. For example the participants narrated how they had to walk in pairs, stand in lines, dress in uniform etc. The participants reported that it was a 'regimented' experience, with no capacity for independent thought or the ability to challenge the dictates inflicted upon them.

One participant (Tina) encapsulated the general feelings expressed by nearly all of the participants' experiences, as having independent thoughts or ideas *'knocked out of you in 4 or 5 years of high school'.* Tina also remarked that because there were no opportunities for diversity she lost interest in her schoolwork all together, and developed a very negative impression of education because it was *'basically all at one level … it is almost like a one size fits all'*.

Several of the participants expressed resentment at having to conform to the expectations of school teachers and society. Some of the participants also voiced their feelings that if you were not one of the teacher's favourites and were not willing to conform to their dictates you were ostracised and 'pushed to the side'. From the conclusions drawn from the interviews it became apparent that being singled out as a non-conforming student instilled feelings of fear and a degree of anxiety.

Teaching Practices, the Banking Concept of Education, Effects upon Teachers.

Looking back, as a participant in this research and reflecting upon by my own teaching practices as an inexperienced new teacher over 20 years ago when I was teaching A Levels, I now ask myself if I 'oppressed' my young and naïve students by literally pumping in the information they needed to gain their qualifications – which was clearly akin to the banking system (Freire, 1996). I question, therefore, what has made me change my teaching practices from using an oppressive banking style, to that of a teacher using a transformational style? This is of course associated with the Research Question 3 (What was it in particular that promoted feelings of empowerment and agency for the Teacher Participants, both during and following their classroom experiences of transformational teaching at Riverside East College as my students? Did the impact of their own student experiences of transformational teaching influence their current teaching practices at the Riverside East College?)

Having now reached a new level of conscientization as a result of the teaching practices I experienced as an Undergraduate, Postgraduate and Doctorate student, I can now see how and why my own teaching practices have been transformed. As an A Level teacher if I had not taught in a banking style my students would probably have failed their exams, as they would not have been given the information considered necessary by the dictates of the academics writing the questions. As A Levels are one of the gateways to employment or Undergraduate studies I had no choice but to dictate the information given to me to replicate, so I think now that I was therefore an oppressor myself in this respect. With respect to the Research Question 3 the teaching practice I had to adopt when teaching A Levels ensured the prevention of my own empowerment and agency within the classroom.

After my initial teaching experiences with A Level students I did progress onto teaching Undergraduates myself. I was then no longer subjected to the necessity of having to pump information into the students within very tight time restrictions dictated by the academics writing questions for an unseen examination.

Critical and Transformational Theory

Freire (1996) makes it quite clear that a 'rebirth', or what I would consider to be a transformational process, is not just about freeing an individual or society from oppressive practices, it is necessary for the oppressed to reflect upon and acknowledge an awareness of their own oppression in order to become an entirely new humanised entity. Freire (1996, p.30) considers that 'This pedagogy makes oppression and its causes objects of reflection by the oppressed, and from that reflection will come their necessary engagement in the struggle for their liberation. And in the struggle this pedagogy will be made and remade'.

From the responses gained during the semi structured interviews it became clear that both as individuals and collectively, a sense of transformation had occurred. Individuals talked of how the course had been *'liberating because it opens up new possibilities'* (8Y1J), and interestingly, in tune with Freire, recognition that the pedagogy is 'made and remade', as one participant commented that *'I'd say I haven't transformed completely, but I'm transforming. I don't think the transition is completely done yet... I am still questioning everything.'* (17Y2C, previously referred to in the findings Chapter 4).

Collectively, the students have challenged and successfully reversed management decisions concerning both staff and academic resources, which they considered not to be in the current or future student population interests. As all of the teachers have themselves been former students upon the course, their own transformations have collectively been transmitted onto their own students, and as such wider society. These collective transformations have been evidenced by the teacher's responses during the interviews. The manner in which the teachers collective transformations are engendered through their interactions with their own students is succinctly summarised by one of the teacher's who commented that *'I hope I am part of an ongoing and growing movement of people who are waking up and realising what is going on … I feel the world needs more action and more people to realise what is going on because no system can last forever and capitalism is a system the same as anything else … We were encouraged to be critical thinkers and in all my lectures I encourage a set of questioning and breaking down of ideas'* (2TTS previously referred to in the findings Chapter 4).

Critical and Transformational Teaching Styles, Influence upon Students

Some of the participants expressed a degree of discomfort, associated with experiencing a critical style of teaching which was linked to Fromm (1961) who talked of the fear of freedom and the awakening of new and innovative ways of learning that impacted directly upon the student's identity. Whether this was a real fear that could be thought of in negative terms or alternatively in a positive fashion in that people became more enlightened to a new form of reality and an enhanced level of awareness is obviously contentious.

It also became abundantly clear that the participants considered they had gained not only an increased awareness of social injustices but in addition a desire and recognition of their own ability to work towards challenging imbalances within society. In this respect the participants clearly felt their own levels of personal agency had increased considerably resulting from the teaching practices they had experienced at the Riverside East College. As many of the participants stated that they intended to work as teachers in the future the research findings indicated that they would instil their concerns about social inequalities into their own students, and as a result engender a sense of personal agency generated by their own teaching practices.

The responses I gave to the prompts used in question 4, (Appendix 4) reflected some of the literature I read and discussed with my teachers and peers in great depth as a Social Science Undergraduate within a College setting, such as Marx, Orwell, Foucault, Freud, and Fromm, to name but a few. Clearly the critical teaching practices I experienced as an Undergraduate, involving in-depth discussions, and responding to problem solving questioning, engendered a desire to learn more and then go on to help others to discover the humanisation of education as a teacher myself.

Critical and Transformational Teaching Styles, Influence upon Teachers

Carol (7TTC) also considered that the way the teaching practices had impacted upon her within the classroom had an effect upon her own teaching in that she stated *'Teaching is not just about telling people stuff. It's about inspiring them to want to find out for themselves... it is like being an enabler rather than a teacher ... and by year 3 they are gone'*. Clearly Carol felt that, like Vincent it is not just about teaching facts it is more about Freire's statement that 'Liberating education consists in acts of cognition, not transferrals of information' (Freire 1996, p.60).

Vincent (3TTV) when asked about whether the teaching practices he had experienced as a student had an impact upon him outside the classroom he replied *'I question everything now and I can't switch off ... I see things behind media campaigns and it's affected me in that it has given me more lateral thinking ... I am able to look at things from lots of different points of view, consider alternatives, and to think about where did those ideas come from? I won't just accept all sorts of things that are told by the media, you know I challenge things out there.'*

Critical, Transformational Teaching, Relationships, Teachers and Students

The reported interactions between school teachers for both male and female participants were also thought of as being key issues emerging from the research in terms of class and gender relationships. One of the male participants, Benny (24PSB) considered that at *'grammar school the subjects I did best at were when I liked the teacher … I seemed to put more effort into it … I absolutely loved the way you taught because you are more like a mother'.*

With regard to the Research Question 3, I agree with Freire (1996, p.30) in that my former experience as an A Level teacher and 'host' to the oppressors has helped me tobe aware of how important the relationship between teachers and learners is, with particular regard to the transformational process. My feelings of empowerment and

233

agency within the classroom now, having developed from my former role, and of my present transformational style of teaching, I can support the metaphor of 'mother' (used by Benny 24PSB) to describe myself, as I consider that I have helped my students to work towards the process of humanisation, rather than dehumanisation.

By contrast however, the responses indicated that if there was very little interaction between the teachers and learners this had a major effect upon levels of interest in the subject matter, feelings of non-agency, and the perception of fearful consequences associated with challenging oppressive practices. One participant, Jess (4TTJS) reported that '*if you have grown up thinking you are stupid*' (then added speaking of her experience at the Riverside East College) … '*you get encouraged that even if you are wrong … everyone's opinion counts … I think that builds up your self-esteem and something I try to give my students … because you don't have to accept all the crap you have been given and told.*' Jess's response and those of several participants indicates the teaching relationships and practices they had experienced at Riverside East College had an impact upon them both inside and outside of the classroom (Research Question 1).

A Fear of Freedom

Fear of teaching in a transformational style was another major factor that was addressed within this research when reviewing the work of Freire and Shor (1986) in particular. This understandable fear of teaching in the transformative style was not however something that became apparent within the Research, as the teachers were not only used to being taught in this manner, they adopted this style themselves when they became teachers. In addition, as several of our students have become teachers themselves, they have continued to adopt this style and share with their own students. In this respect like ripples in a pond my previous students have continued to spread the message that a critical thinking style of teaching has an impact upon the development of personal agency and a desire to challenge oppressive teaching practices and social inequalities.

The participants expressed feelings of anxiety associated with non-conforming outside of the classroom, if they were not part of the 'cool crowd' in terms of dress, hairstyles or parental levels of class and economic security. Certainly as a child coming from a working class background it was very difficult for my parents to be able to afford the expensive school uniform, but as they appreciated how fearful it would be for me not to have this dictated commodity they were prepared to make huge personal sacrifices to obtain it. In this respect the fear of not conforming can be thought of as worse than accepting oppressive and powerful dictates, but it is this fear that we need to overcome in order to take risks and challenge conformity (hooks, 1994).

Whether an increased level of awareness and the confidence to challenge previously held beliefs can be viewed in a negative or positive manner is open to question. For example for Fromm (1961) Freire, (1996), hooks, (1994), these challenges can produce a sense of fear and agitation and an increased level of awareness, which can then generate the desire for an escape route from oppressive practices within society. It could also be proposed that without a sense of anxiety and fear there would be no motivational force to escape any oppressive forces. In other words, perhaps there has to be an element of cognitive dissonance prior to cognitive restructuring, and the need to rethink an unpleasant feeling or situation, or as Freire (1996) may argue the need for praxis and problem solving.

Within the research findings feelings of discomfort were demonstrated and clearly linked to the participants' increased levels of critical awareness (conscientization) of oppressive and powerful structures within society, associated with the fear of freedom talked about by Fromm (1961) in particular.

Pedagogy of Hope, Freedom, and Transformation

Judging from the responses, all of the participants gained an increased level of awareness as to how their interactions within the world could legitimately produce new knowledge and as such a new sense of reality for themselves and others. The responses provided confirmation that the teaching practices at the Riverside East College did, therefore, engender transformational effects in themselves, and a realisation that previous and present powerful forces of domination can be challenged as well.

In particular through transformational educational practices the participants responses supported the statement made by Freire (1996, p.62) that 'Students, as they are increasingly posed with problems relating to themselves in the world and with the world, will feel increasingly challenged and obliged to that challenge'. The frequent reference to the 'world' also supports the Research Question 2, as to whether the transformational teaching practice had an impact upon learners inside and outside of the classroom. Clearly the answer is in the affirmative according to the responses referring to the world generated in the interviews.

Methodology

The rich data gained from the qualitative research validated my ontological position; epistemology and the methodology used in the research, in that I was able to understand and validate the subjective and humanised dialogues and narratives. The use of narrative interviews and semi structured interviews produced clear evidence that the participants had reached a different and more intense level of critical consciousness or 'conscientization', (Freire 1996) resulting from the teaching practices they had experienced at the Riverside East College.

238

The manner in which the research findings were produced could also be strongly linked to the methodology when considered as a form of triangulation, albeit it unintentionally. Ollman (2003, p.12) summarised dialectic methodology as 'is a way of thinking that brings into focus the full range of changes and interactions that occur in the world. As part of this, it includes how to organise a reality viewed in this manner for purposes of study and how to present the results of what one finds to others'. Again it seems that the participants were aware as to how the teaching practices had an impact upon their everyday lives (Research Question 2), as demonstrated by the narratives and responses gained, which explicitly supported the qualitative methodology used.

The narrative responses gained regarding the teaching practices at the Riverside East College were overwhelmingly congruent with the aims of critical thinking advocates and all of the Research Questions. The responses generated a great deal of rich data from the narratives and semi structured questions which fully supported the overall aims of the research and the research design. Following initial coding procedures, (Cycle 1), consideration was given to the impact the teaching practices had within the class room setting, and the impact outside of the classroom (Research Question 1). Table one provided examples of the descriptive data gained from the responses to this question as an initial coding process.

The positive impact the teaching practices had upon the participants upon their overall life and by contrast the negative impact upon their overall life, if any, were explored (Research Question 2). Table two was produced to indicate key words and descriptive responses in order to get a feel of the data and the themes that arose overall.

Metaphor Analysis

One expected bonus that arose from the narratives was the participants' use of metaphors, which provided some very useful and interesting insights into the research data and the methodology employed. Although the use of metaphors had not been thought of as particularly relevant when considering the research design it soon became apparent that this was a 'hidden treasure' and certainly worthy of analysis. As this research is all about how teaching practices can have a transformational effect upon my students, and teachers, after reviewing the transcripts again and again I was pleasantly surprised to see how the use of metaphors related so well to the study of 'Systematic Metaphor Analysis as a Method of Qualitative Research' Schmitt, (2005, p.358).

Although Schmitt, (2005), talks of Cognitive Linguistics (which he attributes to Lakoff and Johnson, 1980, 1999), throughout most of his research I can see how metaphor analysis can work in terms of the latent structures of meaning in the same manner that hooks (1994), Schmitt (2005) speak of. Schmitt (2005, p.358) proposes that 'For almost all qualitative methods of research, language is at one and the same time subject and medium. It is used above all as material referring to content outside language: patterns of relationships, latent structures of meaning, communicative strategies, etc.' Within sociology studies and teaching we do of course consider discourse analysis within research and literature on a regular basis, but I felt that in addition the participants' use of metaphors in my research helped to provide another form of validity and triangulation as part of the qualitative analysis. Schmitt (2005, p.382) agrees with Flick (2000) by stating that 'depending on the question being researched, the triangulation (Flick, 2000) of metaphor analysis with other methods of evaluation is to be recommended.' So in this respect I consider that this unexpected bonus of giving weight to the metaphors used within the narratives had two benefits by providing a basis for a rich analysis of the data, and by validating the methodology used.

Furthermore, as the analysis of metaphors was not part of the original research design I did not consciously set out to look for, or provide participants with metaphors, in order to make any resulting data fit into the Research Questions and questions. As someone who has taught psychoanalysis for several years I could, with hindsight, have deliberately given the participants metaphors to comment upon within the semi- structured interview questions as I consider that I would have had the knowledge and experience to do this. In my research this unintentional and serendipity bonus of obtaining the rich data from the metaphors was, I considered, generated by the participants on an unconscious, rather than conscious level, which I think gave more weight and validity to these responses.

When speaking critically of the previous banking system of education the participants had experienced at school, they then spoke of their present form of enlightenment by using metaphors such as 'seeing the light' etc. In this respect the use of metaphors in the research reflect Schmitt (2005, p.360) who proposed that 'metaphors are not tools, but rather form a structure in which we live… to bring the use of metaphors and the practices associated with this to the conscious level; a mission more of enlightenment which can sometimes be critical of prevalent ideologies'.

The use of metaphors is used liberally within Freire (1996) in order to demonstrate the manner in which he considered that learners gain a sense of awakening and enlightenment (conscientization). 'Time and again, peasants have expressed these discoveries in striking ways after a few hours of class … We were blind, now our eyes have been opened' (Freire 1996. p.15). The comments relating to eyes being opened are reflected several times by my participants' in this research as referred to in Chapter Four. For example when asked about the key themes that had emerged from their teaching experiences (Interview Question 3), 4TTJS remarked that *'I've opened my eyes more to what goes on in the world'*. In addition 15Y2W commented that *'I actually feel as though I was very blinkered before I started the course'*.

The research findings clearly indicated that there were links made between the visionary metaphor of eyes and the feelings of enlightenment associated with their educational experiences upon the course. This point was made succinctly by Saul (2TTS) who stated that '*I feel education should be about enlightening people and waking them up from their mass media coma*'. Vincent (3TTV) also supported this point regarding education and enlightenment by proposing that '*Enlightenment for me is probably the most important thing in education because it's a sense of knowing that there are broader things out there than just the humdrum things in life ... The world just isn't about how much money can we make, it's about enlightening your spirit, your soul ... becoming more of a person and looking at the world through different eyes ... and when you can see it, there's a spark in students, you can see them start to challenge ideas and become a bit more enlightened to alternative viewpoints*'.

Freire also uses the metaphor of a 'rebirth' (1996) which again is reflected within this research. Within my research clear links were made between breaking free from traditional oppressive banking styles of education at school and the liberating 'rebirth' they experienced at the Riverside East College . Freire (1996, p.31) proposes that:

244

'Liberation is thus a childbirth, and a painful one. The man or woman who emerges is a new person, viable only as the oppressor-oppressed contradiction is superseded by the humanisation of all people. Or to put it another way, the solution of this contradiction is born in the labor which brings into the world this new being: no longer oppressor nor longer oppressed, but human in the process of achieving freedom.'

Other examples of metaphors regarding the notion of a rebirth following an increased awareness of oppressive forces and then experiencing the 'humanisation' of knowledge included Wendy, (15Y2W) who stated that *'We're all puppets aren't we? I don't want to be a puppet any more. I've been enlightened and I don't want to be oppressed ... oppression is important, because once you're enlightened you don't want to be shackled, you want to be free ... I think this is something else the course teaches you is to think for yourself, rather than have Society think for you as a collective thought ... I do like that about the course'*.

As referred to in the research findings (Chapter Four) Jack (8Y1J) stated *'it's kind of like a caterpillar turning into a butterfly'*. The metaphor of previously being in *'a bubble of ignorance'* (5TTD) for example was also referred to within the research, and linked to a feeling of safety. Participants in the research clearly felt that when the teaching practices burst their bubble this left them feeling somewhat uncomfortable and fearful concerning the challenges they had felt about their traditionally held beliefs and versions of reality. Angela stated that '*Saul started it, made me think about everything ... he did burst my bubble and I was a little upset by that*' (14Y2A).

The feelings of disquiet expressed by the participants following their own personal conscientization and coming out of the 'bubble of ignorance' were clearly linked to both Freire (1996), Freire and Shor (1986) and Fromm (1961) as referred to in the review of literature (Chapter Two). Uncomfortable feelings were also referred to in response to Interview Question 2 of the research when participants were asked how teaching practices had impacted on their learning in a positive or negative way. For example I responded that I felt '*unsettled*' (1TTJ), Vincent (3TTV) responded that he had '*no switch off*', Ruth (13Y2R) stated that she was more 'cynical', and Angela (14Y2A) commented that she could not '*get it out of my head*'.

Summary of the Thematic Analysis of Findings

I found the analysis of the metaphors, and the qualitative methodology, very rewarding in that the participants provided deep insights into the extent that teaching practices had upon both their educational and social lives. In addition I am absolutely convinced now that a positivist quantitative methodology would have been totally inappropriate for this research. I know that it would have been impossible to extrapolate the rich and valid data concerning real life educational experiences of teaching practices and critical thinking effects, without the interactions between the participants, the narratives, and giving consideration to the associated supporting literature.

Clearly there would have been far too many confounding variables to consider if the research had been dependent upon quantitative methods, such as large scale surveys or multiple choice questions, for example. I consider that the only way it was possible to have gained such in-depth knowledge of how the participants viewed their own versions of reality, both as an individual, and that of society, was to interact with them through the dialogues and narratives of their life and educational experiences.

So, as we approach the last part of our journey together, it is time to reflect upon where this research has taken us, and where it will continue to take us in the future.

Chapter Six, the Conclusions

Introduction

This Research has been all about the educational and transformational journey and the process of all the participants, including mine. Like so many journeys in life there have been times when reflection has been given to the past, historical educational experiences, and then almost like a metaphorical New Year's Eve, attention was given to looking forward to the future with the hope and desire to challenge current undesirable threats to English Universities. These concluding comments, as a form of praxis are therefore written up in a style that is linked to the humanisation of education and as such, like life, full of how the continual interactions between the participants have produced the conclusions drawn.

The Problem Solving Quest of the Research

The quest for this research was to show how teaching in a transformational style had an effect upon both Undergraduate Sociology students and their teachers. The research was also a quest for future research, to demonstrate how transformational teaching practices can work to promote feelings of agency, both within and outside of educational environments.

Pedagogy of Hope

The research was also seen as a pedagogy of hope, in that Holloway (2010) really did show how it was possible for ordinary people, like me, working as a teacher, and thousands of individuals from different walks of life, can 'create a different world…to break the world as it is. A world of injustice … of discrimination … A world ruled by money, ruled by capital … of frustration, of wasted potential' (Holloway, 2010, p.3). This research endorsed the need to 'Crack Capitalism' by showing how critical teaching practices can create a sense of awareness and agency and the belief that there is an alternative to oppressive practices within society. As Amsler et al. point out there is an alternative to this, and that pedagogy of hope can engender a sense of agency rather than the belief that there is no alternative (TINA). The research will make a modest contribution to the existing body of knowledge therefore, with regard to the impact upon students and teachers experiencing a particular style of transformational teaching, associated with critical thinking practices.

The Impact of Critical Teaching Practices

The research has reflected upon, and supported the central problem Freire addressed, with consideration as to how a liberating teaching practice can help learners to challenge the processes of dehumanisation. As Freire, (1996, p.30) proposes:

> 'The central problem is this: How can the oppressed as divided, unauthentic beings, participate in developing the pedagogy of their liberation? Only as they discover themselves to be 'hosts' of the oppressor can they contribute to the midwifery of their liberating pedagogy. As long as they live in the duality in which to be is to be like, and to be like is to be like the oppressor, this contribution is impossible. The pedagogy of the oppressed is an instrument for their critical discovery that both they and their oppressors are manifestations of dehumanisation'.

Class and Gender Issues

Within the research the extensive work of the black feminist writer bell hooks illustrated how a teaching community could help to address class and gender issues. By 'Teaching to Transgress' hooks (1994, p.142) points out that 'Aware of myself as a subject of history, a member of a marginalised and oppressed group, victimised by institutional racism, sexism, and class elitism, I had a tremendous fear that I would teach in a manner that reinforces these hierarchies'. The fears associated with either reinforcing power structures or by contrast challenging them by teaching in a transformational was also addressed within the research, with particular regard to Fromm, (1961), Shor and Freire, (2004).

After listening to the participants' narratives about their previous experiences of education, I felt certain that they had been oppressed to differing extents by their class and gender. As a result during this period they were at Stage One, as proposed by Freire (1996), Sweet, (1998), in that they had not gained an awareness of this form of oppression. After experiencing a form of critical teaching at Riverside East College, however, they seemed to progress to Stage two, as judging from their narratives they had gained an increased awareness of their former oppressive educational experiences.

There was however, something of a contradiction to how the other participants responded regarding their perceptions of school and their experiences of the banking system that Freire talked about. One female student responded that she liked school because of the rules and dictates she experienced at her previous Grammar School. Ruth, (13Y2R) spoke fondly of her previous school and commented that when she went to the Riverside East College to study for her A Levels it was quite unsettling. Ruth stated that 'I cannot say I flourished here in particular, it wasn't really for me as I came from

such a protected environment from an All Girls' Grammar school …
it was very strict - my school uniform wise - you had to even wear
brown knickers as part of the uniform and you had knickers checks.
And then you come here and you could do anything you like so yeah
I think I was a bit naïve and sheltered … it was just a shock coming
here'.

Although throughout this research and data analysis it has become
clear that the participants gained a perceived sense of how they had
been oppressed at school by the teaching practices, rules and
regulations, for this one particular participant, this type of experience
gave her a feeling of security and safety. In addition, when asked if
she found it easier to learn at her previous Grammar school she
remarked 'Yes I did, it was a much more structured environment
than here. … I think it was just the fact that it was just what was
expected. You went to school and the teachers expected you to sit
there and learn. It was Rote, not all of it was Rote, but it was a very
traditional school and you took it down and you reproduced if for
your homework and you were expected to do it. Whereas when I
was doing A' Levels, [at the Riverside East College] the freedom
was a just bit of a shock'.

What however was in tune with all the other participants, including Ruth, and the review of literature was that individuals seem to experience a sense of fear and uncertainty when moving on from oppressive forces, to a sense of empowerment. This seemed to be particularly the case for the female respondents, who talked of feeling safe inside their own little bubble, which was then burst when they experienced teaching practices or when the teachers *'removed their rose tinted glasses when thinking about the world'* (Cathy, 17Y2C).

It also became abundantly clear that the participants' working class versions of reality had been alienated from them by the manner in which they had previously been taught, and the oppressive influences of the middle class values experienced at school. I considered from repeatedly analysing the participant responses that this alienation of values had two major effects, one being that they did not have the confidence to challenge the status quo, and the other being a fatalist perception that to be dominated by these forces was inevitable and not open to challenge. The Research conclusions clearly indicated that this fatalist viewpoint was more associated with the working class females than the male participants.

This conclusion can however be challenged to a certain extent in that apart from one all of the participants thought of themselves as having working class values and there were more females (20) than male participants (7). Nevertheless, there was most definitely a substantial increase in the levels of personal agency identified by the participants after they had experienced a transformational style of teaching at the Riverside East College. The impact that this style of teaching practice had upon the participants in terms of their classroom, educational experiences, and their everyday lives was most definitely supportive of the Research Questions.

As a footnote, and as I am including my reflective and reflexive thought processes throughout this research, I can honestly state that after listening, transcribing, and selecting the responses, I experienced a profound sense of admiration, regarding the participants' determination to break free from the oppressive doctrines and teaching practices they had previously experienced.

The Humanisation of the Curriculum

Within the research the 'humanising of the curriculum' as proposed by Freire (1996) was explored in terms of the transformational effects it had upon individuals as agents of change within society. The conclusions drawn from the research fully supported this claim, and clearly provided information that they considered themselves effective agents of change. The information gained was generated in the form of the participant quotes, and their own liberated voices, which they now felt confident to use.

It was also quite rewarding to see how the participants were able to link their own personal life experiences with the sociological concepts of class and gender issues in particular. The Research conclusions demonstrated that for the participants the curriculum was humanised in that their positionality and life experiences were not thought of in terms of abstract concepts and learning about traditional facts taught in a banking style of education, they were explicitly associated with real people, living in a real world. From the responses gained it was quite apparent that if the teachers did not involve students in discussions and meaningful interactions they lacked interest in the subject matter, as it did not seem relevant to their own experiences of life and the 'world' as they know it.

The Teaching Environment and Transformational effects

With particular reference to the transformational style of teaching the participants had experienced at Riverside East College, there were extremely positive comments made regarding the impact of teaching practices in the classroom. The descriptive coding indicated that words such as excitement, encouragement were uniform throughout the responses. Concerning the responses given in terms of the impact of teaching practices inside the classroom there was a strong evidence that students found 'a voice', in that they were able to speak out and gain a great deal of confidence within the classroom discussions. This level of confidence was particularly prevalent regarding the female participants, who had remarked in their narratives that within family lives and school experiences they did not have either the opportunity, or the confidence to voice their own opinions.

Another major finding concerning the teaching practice they had experienced at the Riverside East College, was that they were able to think in a far more critical fashion than in earlier times. The development of enhanced critical thinking had a major transformational effect and impact for each of the participants that were evidenced in the research findings. The enhancement in critical thinking levels and the increase in levels of confidence clearly engendered feelings of personal agency. This sense of personal agency was directed specifically to the sociological subject matters studied on the course, such as social injustice and as to how political factors had impacted upon both their educational and personal experiences.

This is perhaps something of an ethical debate in that the participants clearly felt empowered by their new sense of critical thinking skills, awareness and enlightenment, but alternatively some of the participants felt they had become more critical of every aspect of their lives. Some of the participants reported that this new and what they considered to be a more cynical view of the world had impacted upon their personal relationships in that they found they became more aware of previous oppressive practices by their friends and family. Others felt they were unable to enjoy simple aspects of their lives such as reading newspapers, watching the news on the TV etc, as they no longer believed anything in a full and contented fashion. These feelings were summarised by one participant who remarked '*I can't switch off anymore*' Vincent (3TTV) and another participant who stated that she had been '*content in her bubble, but after the course she was no longer content and there was no going back as she could not unlearn anymore*' Joan (27PSJ).

The Teaching Environment and the Institutional Barriers of teaching HE in a rural FE College in the UK

Within the introduction to this thesis mention was made as to the lack of HE students from a range of cultural origins and backgrounds due to the geographical and demographic nature of the FE institution, Riverside East College. By contrast, at the University that franchises the course there are much higher numbers of HE students from different cultural backgrounds, and as such provisions are made for a variety of religious requirements such as a quiet room for prayer. Considerations for these requirements are incorporated within the student timetables with respect to religious and cultural needs and desires. Regretfully due to the extremely low numbers of people from a diversity of backgrounds undertaking HE courses at the Riverside East College, the provision of Prayer Rooms, and recognition of dietary and fasting periods that may occur during examination assessment periods is somewhat limited. As referred to in the introduction of this thesis, the students at the Riverside East College from minority groups, may not, therefore feel able to fully engage in the humanised critical thinking processes necessary for transformational processes.

HE students belonging to a minority cultural group, males, and those who have a perceived middle class identity, attending rural FE Colleges and institutions such as the Riverside East College, may also feel quite isolated from the majority of the other students. With regard to the identification classifications and transformational teaching practices talked about in the introduction, regarding the Riverside East College, this may be problematic for both individuals, and the institution itself. If students do feel isolated from the majority of predominately white, working class females they may be reluctant to continue with their studies, and as such the retention rates and the choice of courses available at the FE institution could be affected. Students who had concerns about feeling isolated from the 'University Student Community' were identified within the Runnymede Community Studies research (2007, p.11) where it was reported that;

> 'Students voiced that they were attracted to the SU [State University] for its community reputation and because it was located in a major metropolitan area which embraces differences and diversity. John seemed pleased with his choice, and recounted how alienated a school friend felt at a provincial campus university as a result of its lack of class and ethnic diversity'.

Sims, et al (2007) does therefore emphasise the need for a provision of a variety of social clubs and the ability to live in Halls of Residence as a major requirement for the 'University Student Community' to develop effectively.

Ironically perhaps, much has been made in this thesis concerning the benefits of a small close knit community as an aid to enhance transformational teaching at the Riverside East College, due to the low numbers and the ability to discuss topics such as oppressive behaviours in small groups. ADD QUOTE As to whether the institutional barriers associated with low number of HE students at FE institutions, or the high numbers of students coming from a diverse social and cultural background has an effect upon transformational teaching practices is therefore debatable, and worthy of future research perhaps.

In addition, for HE teachers working in FE there could be institutional barriers to transformational teaching practices due to reduced, or minimal funding for academic contemporary research and sabbaticals. On a practical level, with a limited number of teachers working on HE programmes in FE Colleges, to release individuals for a sabbatical may also be an institutional barrier that inhibits scholarly research. Furthermore within FE institutions, the teaching contact hours are likely to be considerably more than those within HE institutions, and include teaching on different levels of programmes as well. Parry et al (2012, p.53) state that;

> 'Staff who teach higher education courses in FECs usually have longer contact hours than their counterparts in HEIs but the programmes taught in colleges might have more contact hours overall. The size of their classes is mostly smaller than the audiences taught in lecture halls and seminar groups in most universities. Many college lecturers and tutors teach on both higher education and further education courses'.

Institutionally therefore, for HE teachers working in FE, the increased contact hours may reduce their motivation and ability to teach in an innovative transformational style, and necessitate teaching in a more banking style involving 'death by PowerPoint'. If, however the HE students studying at the Riverside East College do have more hours attributed to their programme as Parry (2012) suggests, this would give them more opportunities to engage in the small group discussions associated with transformational teaching practices.

Political Awareness

Although an individual's versions of reality are likely to change and develop due to maturation, life events, social relationships etc.

the participants clearly considered that for them personal major changes had occurred as a result of the teaching practices experiences they had received at Riverside East College. One of the most important changes they reported was that they had become more politically aware of the effects of capitalism and neoliberalism in their everyday lives and within the classroom. Whether these changes could be mainly affiliated with the teaching practices or the subject matter is of course open to question.

On reflection, and with consideration to the key words used in the Interview question 4, which are all related to aspects of political and sociological study, this begs the question as to whether the teaching style the participants experienced was the dominant factor responsible for any transformational effects, or was it the subject matter? My research does not attempt to answer this question, but to recognise that it is clear from the interviews and other sociological research in this area that the content of the sociological degree is an important factor in terms of transformation and empowerment of teachers and learners, Ashwin and Abbas (2013). In this research I have chosen to focus on teaching practices and have found that they do make a significant difference to the students enhanced level of

263

awareness of social injustices and oppressive practices within society. As shown in the responses gained the students indicated that they had become more politically aware of both personal levels of oppression at school, and adulthood in the UK and globally. Furthermore, the participants responses indicated that the teaching practices they had experienced upon the degree had motivated and enhanced their sense of agency to challenge and act to address their concerns.

Transferability of critical, transformational pedagogy to alternative disciplines

With further consideration, as the Riverside East College participants demonstrated advanced levels of critical thinking when discussing other topics and disciplines such as psychology and criminology, I think it is fair to assume that the transformational style of teaching was the dominating factor rather than the subject of political sociology. The students also demonstrated problem solving behaviours (Freire, 1996) when asked to work collectively to develop group presentations and produce posters for criminology, and psychology assessments which again indicates that the transformational style of teaching generated a sense of personal empowerment and agency across disciplines.

Transformational and critical thinking teaching practices have also been used successfully when applied to diverse subjects and disciplines such as mathematics and music tuition. For example authors of the Journal of Urban Mathematics Education (Vol 9, No 1 (2016) claim 'The mission of the journal is to foster a transformative global academic space in mathematics that embraces critical research, emancipatory pedagogy, and scholarship of engagement in urban communities' Abrahams (2005, p.6) also provides a clear demonstration as to how critical pedagogy can effectively applied to other disciplines such as the teaching of music by stating that;

> 'Critical pedagogy views teaching such that the teacher, like the music critic, acts as the discriminating musical connoisseur and places information into a context that is familiar to the student. The classroom activities further students' musicianship and enable them as musicians who think, act and feel at intense levels. Music teachers who teach critically view themselves in a partnership with the students. As a result, they experience outcomes that are personally transformational.'

Allman (2010) and teaching colleagues, conducted a study working with participants' (described as learning colleagues) who came from diverse educational backgrounds, who might have become Freirean educators in the future. Allman, (2010, p.182) reflected on these academic diversities by commenting that 'In other courses offering the same or similar awards, students normally study adult and community education from a variety of disciplinary perspectives, including psychology, philosophy, sociology, history and sometime, but not often, political economy'. With respect to these subject diversities Allman (2010) considered that all of the participants, including the Freirean educators themselves should take responsibility for developing a 'theme' to study. This choice of theme then had to be studied intensively by the educators in order to provide some relevant resources for the participants, although as Allman (2010, p.180) points out;

> 'It would have been infinitely simpler to predetermine the themes and have all the resources selected and to hand prior to the commencement of the course. However …we felt it important to draw themes from what was currently of central concern to learning colleagues in a particular group … we thought it vitally important to select the themes in concert with the group … we thought this was important … our learning colleagues were also learning how to engage in Freirean education- learning how to become Freirean educators'.

Allman's research does therefore indicate that Freirean educators can use this form of teaching practice within a wide variety of disciplines, rather than exclusively linked to one such as sociology for example, as focused upon in my research. Allman, (2010, p.180) also states that 'the curriculum for the course was always based on "generative themes" – that is, Freire's idea of a theme or issue that is central to and manifested in the lives of the participants'. Allman supports this claim further with a quote from Freire, (1972 pp.68-95) 'Through the co-investigation of generative themes, people learn to "read" their world critically'. In my research the 'theme' of looking at critical thinking teaching practices associated with a sociology undergraduate course, and reflecting upon how it helped 'people learn to "read" their world critically' (ibid), can be effectively demonstrated as closely following Freirean educationalists and Allman's work.

Metaphor Analysis and Insights

The identification and interpretation of metaphors provided deep and meaningful insights into the impact of participants' educational experiences and as such adherence to the exploration of the Research

Questions. Craib (2001) argues that although Freud proposed the psychological development of an individual involved the same type of journey, the manner in which the person travels can be dependent upon different life experiences. In this respect I concluded that the manner in which Freire (1996) and the participants, narrated their educational experiences via metaphors, validated the interpretation and the analysis of the metaphorical language used throughout the research. As Craib (2001, p.47) considers:

> 'Our psychological development can best be seen as finding a path through a possibly dangerous forest, but one with lots of animal tracks that we can follow. We all have to go through the forest, but each of us has to find his or her own way and that will be different from everybody else's. So our development will be different depending on our culture, our social class and our family history: it will also vary with the internal conscious and unconscious metaphors and interpretations by means of which we try to make sense of our experience'.

When attempting to make sense of the information and research data I concluded that the metaphors used reflected the participants' positionality, including my own, in terms of social class, family history and gender. The interpretation of the metaphors were in most cases somewhat self-explanatory, although some were open to debate, and dependent upon my own analysis, which again could be associated with my own positionality. In some respects therefore the subjective interpretation of some of the more ambivalent metaphors could have limitations regarding the validity of this form of data analysis.

However, as so many of the participants used very similar metaphors within their narratives to describe their journey through their educational experiences, I concluded that this form of discourse analysis provided lots of evidence concerning the 'animal tracks' we followed together during the interviews. Indeed even the metaphorical reference to the 'possibly dangerous forest' could be interpreted as the fears and risks often referred to by Freire (1996), Freire and Shor (1989), Fromm (1961), hooks (1994) and the participants when associated with transformational teaching practices and educational experiences.

The Research Questions

The conclusions drawn from the participants' responses, and the review of my own reflective thoughts concerning teaching practices has addressed the Research Questions, the development of which was a process of problem solving in itself.

From the narratives and interview responses the Banking Style of teaching (Freire, 1996) had a restrictive impact upon the participants' attitudes of empowerment and agency. From the responses gained it would seem that school experiences were thought of in very negative terms. Although the Interview Question 1 asked about the experiences since leaving school, it was clear that the participants were comparing the transformational teaching practices they had experienced at Riverside East College, Degree or Access, with that of school. The participants own comparisons between school and HE teaching practices provided enlightenment, clarity, and effectively addressed the Research Questions. By contrast the manner in which the participants were taught in a transformational style demonstrated how this had a liberating and empowering impact upon the participants (Research Question 1)

The Research findings and conclusions in this chapter demonstrate which particular aspects of the transformational teaching experiences either promoted or restricted the student's attitudes of empowerment and agency. The responses gained from all three groups of participants, (current and former students, and the teachers) provide an analytical review as to how and when the transformational changes actually occurred (Research Question 2).

Conclusions as to how the teaching practices experiences the teachers received previously either restricted, or enhanced their own sense of empowerment and agency were reviewed. The conclusions drawn also demonstrate how the critical style of teaching they received on the Sociology Course as students, influenced their own practice as teachers on the same course. In addition, the manner in which I was taught in a transformational style as an Undergraduate in a College demonstrates the attitudes of empowerment, and the limitations of personal agency I currently experience as a teacher at the Riverside East College (Research Question 3).

Strengths and Limitations of the Research

One of the major strengths of the research was the qualitative methodology, including the selection of participants. By looking at the same FE College delivering HE the participant teachers themselves had all been taught Sociology by myself, and as such were used to being taught in a transformational style of teaching practice. In this sense because they were able to see the benefits of this style of teaching practice in their own personal and educational experiences, they were able to reproduce and share the same advantages with their own students. Furthermore they were able to recognise, and empathise with students if they expressed symptoms of anxiety and fearwhen asked to partake in group discussions or produce presentations for assessments as they were already aware of those lacking in high levels of self-confidence.

By interviewing the teachers, current students, and former students another strength of this research was that it had some of the beneficial effects of a longitudinal study, in that the effects of teaching in a transformational style over at least 20 years could be reviewed. Having worked at Riverside East College for a period of 20 years I was able to see that the students I had previously taught still maintained the same levels of concern with regard to social issues, such as inequalities in class, gender and racial issues. Furthermore it became clear that they considered they had not only enjoyed being taught in a transformational style they felt they had a duty to challenge social inequalities and had gained increased levels of self-confidence and agency to do this. (Research Question 3).

The extensive review of relevant research was also considered to be a key strength of the research. By looking at a wide range of critical educational theorists and teachers, who had actually worked as teachers themselves, the literature provided humanised and contextualised valid information to base the research upon.

However, as this small scale research was conducted in one particular location, it could be suggested that this is something of a unique situation that may not necessarily be thought of as representative of all FE Colleges where HE teaching takes place. In addition, as with any research, but particularly so with qualitative research perhaps, it is impossible to exactly replicate the same environmental conditions, health and disposition of both the researcher and participants. Bryman, (2012, p. 405) makes the point that:

> 'replication in the social sciences is by no means a straight forward matter regardless of the issue ... In qualitative research, the investigator him - or herself is the main instrument of data collection, so that what is observed and heard and also what the researcher decides to concentrate upon are very much products of his or her predilections'.

Another limitation might be that as I have known and taught all of the teachers and students for several years, and as we have worked together in a small community of learners, it is possible that the relationships I had with the participants could have been influential; in that their responses were made according to what they thought *I wanted to know*. Although again, I consider that this possible limitation is not unique to this particular research, and indeed it could be argued that, by contrast, as the participants knew me well, and trusted my integrity they were more likely to have the confidence to respond in a frank and truthful manner.

I consider that the participants would have had no hesitation in giving responses that did not necessarily support the Research Questions if they perceived this was their version of reality. Within class discussions the participants have shown the confidence to make comments that are both frank and forthright regarding the sensitive and controversial topics covered on the programme, as we encourage them to challenge dominating ideologies and examples of oppressive behaviours. I also think that the narrative life stories the participants provided were a considered and comprehensive account of their educational experiences, which they illustrated in depth with examples of events and behaviours.

While I do not make positivistic claims of validity for my research I do feel that it is reliable, creditable and trustworthy (Guba and Lincoln 2004). I make this claim based on the methods I have used to corroborate and confirm the research through the ways in which I have collected data and the theoretical context for the study. Within this research I have used narrative life stories, responses to semi structured interview questions, prompts, descriptive coding of responses, thematic analysis to explore the themes that arose, and the analysis of metaphorical dialogues, in order to produce and confirm the Research Questions had been fully addressed. As a result of this wide variety of data collection and analysis, I have come to the conclusion and confirmation that critical teaching practices have had

275

a transformational effect upon both teachers and learners at the Riverside East College.

I have already discussed the issue about the extent to which the relationship between the content of a sociology curriculum and teaching practices may have an effect upon the data collected. I recognise that the content is a significant factor, this is clear from my interviews and from other literature (Abbas, Ashwin and McClean 2012, 2013), but I have chosen to focus on the teaching practices, inspired by the work of Paula Allman (2010) and others.

The End of this Journey, my Final Reflective and Reflexive comments

In order to explore the Research Questions it has been necessary to travel a long journey with the participants. At times it has been difficult to see where the Research was going but now I can see how all the pieces are starting to fit together like a jigsaw of my life and those of my students, both past and present. Sometimes it has been hard to start again after I have looked back at the writing up of this Research, and then felt it necessary to hold my finger down on the delete button. Writing and conducting this Research has been a process, but the reality is I have lived this educational process every

276

day since I became a teacher 24 years ago, so I am confident that given my methodological framework and methods this research is credible, reliable and trustworthy.

I have shared the excitement of teaching in a transformational style since the very beginning, but it is not over yet, in fact as part of my praxis I see it as the beginning of a new adventure. True to say I am fearful as to how this Research will be viewed, but I also know that this has been a lived and humanised educational experience so the reality is I have been true to my beliefs, and that there is a pedagogy of hope for the future. I know that I am far from alone in my quest to fight against this current crisis in Undergraduate education. As Holloway says there are so many people out there living and working as teachers and academics challenging the educational crisis facing them in England and all over the world. Critical thinkers such as Allman, Amsler, Bovill, Canaan, Freire, Fromm, hooks, Holloway, McLaren, Neary, Roggero, and Sweet have given us enlightenment of the past and present, and hope for the future. I hope that in a small way I have added to this list of individuals who believe that change is always possible.

I have always believed that for me, the best and most effective way to challenge inequalities is through transformational education. So this research has been built on the shoulders of critical thinkers who have endeavoured to give hope to those who have experienced inequalities within society. As Freire acknowledges, (1996, p.3) 'To the oppressed, and to those who suffer with them and fight at their side' is the reason I believe transformational teaching can give us hope for the future.

I will leave the last quote to Freire (1993, p.98) therefore; whose work has inspired me and so many other teachers, both past, present, and who, I am sure, will continue to do so in the future.

> 'This capacity to always begin anew, to make, to reconstruct, and to not spoil, to refuse to bureaucratise the mind, to understand and to live a process- live to become- is something that always accompanied me throughout life. This is an indispensable quality of a good teacher'.

Bibliography

Abbas, A., McLean, M., and Ashwin, P., (2012). *Neoliberal policy, quality and inequality in undergraduate degrees*. In: *Organising Neoliberalism*. Anthem Press, pp. 179-199.

Abrahams, F. (2005)*The application of critical pedagogy to music teaching and learning. Visions of Research in Music Education, 6.* Retrieved from http://www.rider.edu/~vrme [Accessed 20.08.2016]

Adler, P., A., and Adler, P., (1987). *Membership roles in field research*. Newbury Park, CA: Sage.

Allman, P., (2010). *Critical Education against Global Capitalism. Karl Marx and Revolutionary Critical Education.* Rotterdam: Sense Publishers.

Allman, P. (1994) *Paulo Freire's Contributions to Radical Adult Education* The
Critical Pedagogy Reader (Second Edition) London and New York, Routledge.

Amsler, S., Canaan, J., E., Cowden, S. Motta, S., Singh (2010) *Why critical pedagogy and popular education matter today:* Higher Education Academy Subject Network for Sociology, Anthropology, Politics.

Amsler, S. (2011) *Revalorising the Critical Attitude for Critical Education.* Aston University, Birmingham U.K.

Amsler, S. (2015) *The Education of Radical Democracy.* London and New York, Routledge.

Ashwin, P., Abbas, A., and McLean, M., 2012. *The pedagogic device: sociology, knowledge practices and teaching-learning processes.* In: Trowler, P., Saunders, M. and Bamber, V., eds. *Tribes and Territories in the 21st Century.* London: New York: Routledge, pp. 118-129.

Ashwin, P., Abbas, A., McLean, M., (2013) *How do student's accounts of sociology change over the course of their Undergraduate Degrees?* Higher Education eprints.lincoln.ac.uk/11891 [Accessed 20.09.2013]

Barbour, R., S., and Kitsinger, J., (1999). *Developing Focus Group Research. Politics Theory and Practice* London: Sage.

Barthes, R., (1966). *Introduction to the Structural Analysis of the Narrative Occasional Paper, Centre for Contemporary Cultural Studies*. Birmingham: University of Birmingham Press.

Barton, A., C., Louis, K., S., (2002). *Tales from the Science Education Crypt: A Critical Reflection of Positionality, Subjectivity, and Reflexivity in Research*. Forum: Qualitative Social Research, Volume 3, No 3 (2002) [Accessed 02.04.2016]

Bernstein, B., (1971). *Class, Codes and Control (Volume 1)* London: Routledge and Kegan Paul.

Bernstein, B., (2000). *Pedagogy, Symbolic Control and Identity*. London: Rowman and Littlefield Publishers.

Bogdan, R., & Taylor, S., (1975). *Introduction to qualitative research methods*. New
York: John Wiley.

Boreo, G., Pozzi, F. Roggero, G. *Conricerca* as Political Action Available at www.sycamoreprojects.com [Accessed 11.05.2014]

Bovill, C., (2009) *Experimental thoughts*. Available at https://mincedmorsels.wordpress.com [Accessed 11.03.2016]

Bovill, C. (2010) *Students as co-creators of curricula: re-imagining relationships, ownership and practice*. Available at Scholar.google.co.uk [Accessed 12.01.2014]

Bovill, C., Cook-Sather, A., and Felten, P. (2011) *Students as co-creators of teaching approaches, course design, and curricula: implications for academic developers. International Journal for Academic Development.* 16 (2), 133–45. [Accessed 11.03.2016]

Bovill, C., (2011) *Sharing Responsibility for Learning Through Formative*
Evaluation: Moving to Evaluation as Learning.Practice and Evidence of Scholarship of Teaching and Learning in Higher Education Vol. 6, No. 2, October 2011, pp. 96-10 [Accessed 11.03.2016]

Bryman, A., (2012) *Social Research Methods (4th Edition)* Oxford University Press Inc., New York.

Canaan, J., E., (2013) *Where did Class go, Why may it be returning? A view from Sociology students* Birmingham City University, Birmingham, England
Journal for Critical Education Policy Studies, v11 n1 p27-48 Mar Available at http://www.jceps.com/archives/420 [Accessed 22. 06. 2015]

Canaan, J. E., (2013) Transcript: Joyce Canaan interview for Cultural Studies archive 2013 [Accessed 11.10.2015]

Clarke, S., (1991) *Marx, Marginalism and Modern Sociology.* *https://libcom.org/* [Accessed 13.01.2014]

Coffey, A., and Atkinson, P., (1996) *Making Sense of Qualitative Data.Complimentary Research Strategies* London: Sage.
Conti, A,. Curcio, A., De Nicola, A., Paolo, D., Fredda, S., Emiletti, M., Orasi,   S., Roggero, G. Sacco, D. Visco, G. (2007) *The Anamorphosis of Living LabourTheory & politics in*

*organisation,*Available at www.ephemeraweb.org volume 7(1): 78-87 [Accessed 12.01.2015]

Craib, I.,(2001) *Psychoanalysis: A Critical Introduction,* Cambridge: Polity.

Cresswell, J., W., (2003) Research Design Qualitative Quantitative and Mixed Methods Approaches Second Edition pdf. London: Sage Publications

Cresswell, J., W., (2007) *Qualitative Inquiry and Research Design. Choosing Among Five Approaches,* Second Edition. pdf. London: Sage Publications.

Darder, A., Baltodano, Marta, P. and Torres, D., (2009). *The Critical Pedagogy Reader.* 2nd ed. Oxon: Routledge.

Davies, P., (1999). What is evidence-based education? *British Journal of EducationalStudies,* 47(2), pp. 108-121.Available at www.tandfonline.com [Accessed 11.04.2016]

Dunne, E., and Owen, D., (2013). *The Student Engagement Handbook: Bingley*: Emerald Group Publishing Ltd.

Eaton, J., (2015) Students and Scholarship: Why it Matters… available at www.aoc.co.uk/july-2015 [Accessed 04.01.2016]

Erikson, E., H., (1968b).*Identity: Youth and Crisis.* New York: Norton.

Foster, J., B., McChesney, R.W. Jonna, R.J. (2011) *The Global Reserve Army of Labor and the New Imperialism* (Volume 63, Issue 06 (November) [Accessed 01.05.2016]

Fraenkel, J., R., and Wallen, N., E., (2010). *How to design and Evaluate Research in Education.* New York: McGraw-Hill International.

Freire, P., (1993) *Pedagogy of the City.* New York: Continuum.

Freire, P., (1994). *Paulo Freire and Higher Education* Albany, NY: State University of New York Press.

Freire, P., (1996). *Pedagogy of the Oppressed.* London: Penguin Books Ltd.

Freire, P., (1998) *Teachers as cultural workers: Letters to those who dare to teach.* Boulder, CO: Westview.

Fromm, E., (1961). *The Fear of Freedom.* London: Routledge.

Gadotti, M., (1994). *Reading Paulo Freire.* Albany, NY: State of University of New York Press.

Guardian Newspaper Sunday 4th August 2013 *Zero-hours contract workers - the new reserve army of labour?*

Gerke, M., (2013) *The Sociology Classroom: Critical, Transformative, Radical? Part 1 of 3. Problems with Learner-Centered Models.* Sociology Lens.

Gerke, M., (2013) *The Sociology Classroom: Critical, Transformative, Radical? Part 2 of 3. Problems with Learner-Centered Models.* Sociology Lens.

Gibbs, G., (2010). *Dimensions of Quality York*:Higher Education Academy.

Gillborn, D., Mirza, H.S. (2000), Educational *Inequality Mapping Race, Class and Gender, A synthesis of research evidence.* Institute of Education Middlesex University, University of London. Available at www.ofsted.gov.uk [Accessed 16/04/16]

Giroux, H., (1983) *Critical Theory and Educational Practice.* The Critical Pedagogy Reader. 2nd ed. Oxon: Routledge.

Giroux, H., Lankshear, C., Mclaren, P. and Peters, M., (1996). *Counter Narratives Cultural Studies and Critical Pedagogies in Postmodern Spaces.* London: Routledge.

Giroux, H., (2001). *Theory and Resistance in Education: Towards a Pedagogy for the Opposition*. Connecticut, USA: Greenword Publishing Group.

Guba and Lincoln (2005) cited in *Qualitative Validity* Available at www.socialresearchmethods.net/kb/qualval.php [Accessed 15.05.2016]

Hakim, C., (1982). *Secondary Analysis in Social Research: A Guide to Data Sources and Methods with Examples*. London: Allen and Unwin.

HEA (2014) *Framework for partnership in learning and teaching*. Higher Education Academy. Available from: www.heacademy.ac.uk/students-as-partners [Accessed 14.12.2015]

Healey, M., Flint, A. Harrington, K. (2014*) Engagement through Partnership* Available at www.heacademy.ac.uk [Accessed 10.03.2016]

Holloway, J., (2010). *Crack Capitalism*. London: Pluto Press.
hooks, b., (1994). *Teaching to Transgress Education as the Practice of Freedom*. London: Routledge.

Jenkins, C., Canaan, J., Filippakou, O., and Strudwick, K., (2011) *The troubling concept of class: reflecting on our 'failure' to encourage sociology students to re-cognise their classed locations using autobiographical method.* ELiSS, 3(3), 1-30. [Accessed 11.04.2015]

Journal of Urban Mathematics Education (Vol 9, No 1 (2016) Retrieved from http://ed-osprey.gsu.edu/ojs/index.php/JUME [Accessed 20.08.2016]

Kats, J., S., and Martin, B., R., (1995) *What is Research Collaboration?* University of Sussex, Brighton, Falmer.

Macrine, S., Maclaren, P., Hill, D., (2010) *Revolutionising Pedagogy, Education for Social Justice Within and Beyond Global Neo- Liberalism. Hampshire,* Palgrave Macmillan.

Mackenzie, N., Knipe, S., (2006), *Research dilemmas: Paradigms, methods and methodology.* Issues in Educational Research, Vol 16, 2006 Available at www.iier.org.au [Accessed 16.03.2016]

Marx, K., (1867). *Capital: Volume 1.* As Published (2013) Ware, Hertfordhire. Wordsworth Editions Ltd.

Mason, J., (1996). *Qualitative Researching.* London: Sage.

McLaren, P., (2006). *Rage and Hope. Interview with Peter McLaren on War, Imperialism, and Critical Pedagogy.* New York: Lang.

McLean, M., Abbas, A.<http://opus.bath.ac.uk/view/person_id/9697.html> and Ashwin, P., 2013. University knowledge, human development and pedagogic rights.<http://opus.bath.ac.uk/47519/> In: Boni, A. and Walker, M., eds. Human development and capabilties. Routledge, pp. 30-43.

Morgan, H., (1997). *Motivation of Sixth –form Students.* London: Teacher Training Agency.

Neary, M., and Winn, J., (2009). *Student as Producer: reinventing the student experience in higher education* eprints.lincoln.ac.uk. [Accessed 11.07.2012]

Neary, M., with Winn, J., (2009) *Student as producer: Reinventing the Undergraduate curriculum.* In: M. Neary, H. Stevenson, and L. Bell (Eds) (2009) *The future of higher education: Policy, pedagogy and the student experience* (pp. 192–210). London: Continuum. [Accessed 11th July 2012]

Neary, M., (2010). *Student as producer: Research engaged teaching and learning at the University of Lincoln User's Guide 2010-11* [Internet]. Lincoln: University of Lincoln.

Neary, M., et al. (2010). *Learning Landscapes in Higher Education* Centre of Educational Research and Development. Lincoln UK. University of Lincoln.

Neary, M. (2011). Student as producer: Reinventing HE through Undergraduate research [Internet]. *Guardian Higher Education Network*, 22 September 2011.
Neary, M., (2011). Teaching Politically: Policy, Pedagogy and the New European University. *The Journal for Critical Education Policy Studies*. http://www.jceps.com/ [Accessed 18.02.2013].

Neary, M., (2012). *Student as producer: An institution of the common? [or how to recover communist/revolutionary science]*. York: Higher Education Academy. www.heacademy.ac.uk/resources/detail/subjects/csap/eliss/ELISS_v ol4 issue3guestpaper [Accessed 16 June 2014]
Neary, M., Stevenson, H., and Bell, L., (2012). *Towards Teaching in Public. Reshaping the Modern University*. London: Continuum.
Newton, N., (2010). *Exploring Qualitative Methods*. Available from: https://www.academia.edu/1561689/The_use_of_semi-structured_interviews_in_qualitative_research_strengths_and_weakn esses [Accessed 15.05.2016]
NUS and QAA (2012) *Student experience research 2012. Part 1: Teaching and learning: Student experience research to gain insight into the quality of the learning experience* London: National Union of Students. Available from: www.nus.org.uk_NUS_QAA_Teaching_and_Learning.pdf [Accessed 14.05.2014]
Ollman, B., (2003). *Dance of the Dialectic: Steps in Marx's Method*. University of Illinois Press.

Olson, D., H., (1977). *Insiders and outsiders views of relationships: research studies.* In: G, Levinger. and H.L. Rausch, ed. (1977). *Close relationships: perspectives on the meaning of intimacy.* Amhurst: University of Massachusetts Press.

Parry, G., Callender, C., Scott, P., Temple, P., (2012) *Understanding Higher Education in Further Education Colleges*: BIS Research Paper Number 69. PDF [Accessed 25.08.2016]

Robertson, S., (2007). *'Remaking the World': Neo-liberalism and the Transformation of Education and Teachers' Labour*[Accessed 04-02-2016]

Robson, C., (2002). *Real World Research, Second Edition*, Oxford: Blackwell Publishing.

Rocco, T., S., Plakhotnik, M., S.,(2009). *Literature Reviews, Conceptual Frameworks, and Theoretical Frameworks: Terms, Functions, and Distinctions*
Human Resource Development Review Vol. 8, No. 1 March 2009 120-130
Available from hrd.sagepub.com at University of Lincoln [Accessed 18.12.2015]

Roggero, G., (2009). *The Power of Living Knowledge Crisis of the Global University, Class Struggle and Institutions of the Commoneipcp.net* [Accessed 24.03.2012]

Roggero, G., (2011). *The Production of Living Knowledge.* Philadelphia, Temple University Press.

Roggero, G., (2012). *Building Up an Institution of the Common Edufactory.* [Accessed 14.03.2012]

Rustin, M., The biographical turn. In Chambererlayne, P, Bornat, J and Waengraf, T (eds) The Turn to Biographical Methods in the Social Sciences. London, Routledge.

Ryckman, R., M., (2004). *Theories of Personality* Eighth Edition, Maine: Thomson Wadsworth.

Saldana, J., (2009). *The Coding Manuel for Qualitative Researchers* London UK, Sage Publications Ltd

Sapsford, R., and Jupp, V., (2006) *Data Collection and Analysis* Second Edition, London, Sage.

Savin-Baden, M., (2008). *Learning Spaces: Creating Opportunities for Knowledge Creation in Academic Life* Society for Research into Higher Education and Open University Press, Maidenhead and New York.

Savin-Baden, M., and Howell Major, C., (2013). *Qualitative Research The essential guide to theory and practice* London: Routledge.

Shaull (1996) within Freire (intro) Freire, P., (1996). *Pedagogy of the Oppressed.* London: Penguin Books Ltd.

Shor, I., and Freire, P., (1987). *What are the Fears and Risks of Transformation? APedagogy for Liberation: Dialogues on Transforming Education.* Westport, USA: Greenwood Publishing Group.

Sikes, P., and Gale, K., (2006). *Narrative Approaches to Education ResearchUniversity of Plymouth* [Accessed 22.11.2010]

Sims, J., M., (2007). *Not Enough Understanding? Student Experiences of Diversity in UK Universities* Runnymede Trust [Accessed 06.08.2016]

Sipe, L., R., and Ghiso, M., P., (2004). *Developing conceptual categories in classroom descriptive research: Some problems and possibilities. Anthropology and Education Quarterly*, 35 (4), pp. 472-85.

Schmitt, R., (2005). *Systematic Metaphor Analysis as a Method of Qualitative Research.* The Qualitative Report Volume 10, Number 2, June pp 358-394 [Accessed 22.08.2015]

Stake, R., E., (1995). *The Art of Case Study Research.* London: Sage.

Steger, M., B., and Ravi, K.R., (2010). *Neoliberalism A Very Short Introduction.* Oxford: University Press.

289

Sterling, B., (1998). Distraction. USA, Bantam Books.

Stuart, M., (2012). *Social Mobility and Higher Education: The life experiences of first generation entrants in Higher Education.* Stoke on Trent: Trentham Books.

Sweet (1998) In Gerke, M. (2013) *The Sociology Classroom: Critical, Transformative, Radical? Part 1 of 3. Problems with Learner- Centered Models.* Sociology Lens.

Tesch, R., (1990). *Qualitative research: Analysis types and software tools.* London: Falmer.

Tritschler, P., (2016). What's the point of Education? *Transformation, where love meets social justice* [Accessed 01.05.2016]

Trochim, M., K., (2006). *Qualitative Validity.* Available from:http://www.socialresearchmethods.net/kb/qualval.php [Accessed 15.05.2016]

Tronti, M., (1966). Operai e capital 2nd exp.ed., Einaudi Turin Italy.

Walford, G., (2001). *Doing Qualitative Educational Research. A personal guide to the research process.* London: Continuum.

Walker, R., (1985). *Doing Research. A Handbook for Teachers.* London: Methuen.

Watson, D., (2012). The University and its student community: knowledge as transformation? In: P. Temple, ed. *Universities in the Knowledge Economy: Higher Education Organisation and Global Change.* London: Routledge. pp. 197 -211.

Whyte, W., F., (1981). *Street Corner Society: The Social Structure of an Italian Slum.* 3rd ed., Chicago, IL: University of Chicago Press.

Woolf, V., (2008). *A Room of One's Own and Three Guineas* M.Shiach (ed), Oxford World's Classics, Open University Press, Buckingham.

Worthington (2010). as in'*Learning Landscapes in Higher Education.'*

Wright, N., (1989). *Assessing Radical Education* Milton Keynes: Open University Press.

Appendices Section

Appendix One

Table One Cycle 1 of the coding process

Appendix Two

Table two demonstrates the coding for Participants (names anonymised)

Appendix Three

Table Three Demonstrates the descriptive responses to Interview Question 1: 'Tell me about your experience of education since leaving school please'

Appendix Four

Table FourRepresentative Examples of Descriptive Responses arising from Interview Question 2'Tell me how teaching practices have impacted on your learning inside and outside of class – in a positive and negative way'.

Appendix Five

Table FiveResponses given by all participants to key words (prompts) Interview Question 4.I have a list of words that describe the themes I think are important regarding student learning experiences which I would like to share and discuss with you. But before we discuss these themes would you rank them in order of what you think are the most important please?'

Appendix Six

Table SixSummary and Overview of all responses given to the key words (prompts) used in Interview Question 4

Appendix Seven

My transcript produced from the interview questions

Appendix One

Table One

The following table demonstrates Cycle 1 of the coding process

Code   Key descriptive words or phrases

Code	Key descriptive words or phrases
RA1	Research Aim. Teaching Practice- Empowerment HE/FE
RA2	Research Aim. Teaching Practice- Empowerment in life
RA3	Research Aim. Teaching Practice- Empowerment -agency
Q1	Narrative- Previous Teaching/Learning positive + negative
Q2	Narrative- Present Teaching Practices positive + negative
Q3	Narrative- Present Teaching/L - Key Themes gain/arising
Q4	Word Prompts – Results produced in Table Format
Q5D	Question 5 -Consideration of Prompt 1 Democracy
Q5O	Question 5 -Consideration of Prompt 2 Oppression
Q5E	Question 5 -Consideration of Prompt 3 Equality
Q5F	Question 5 -Consideration of Prompt 4 Freedom
Q5T	Question 5 -Consideration of Prompt 5 Transformation
Q5EL	Question 5 -Consideration of Prompt 6 Enlightenment

Q6SI	Consideration of Narrative -Question 6a – Student Identity
Q6TP	Consideration of Narrative -Question 6b – Teaching Practice
MM	Consideration of Metaphors used by participants
DAF	Descriptive -Age Factors
DEF	Descriptive -Ethnicity Factors
DGF	Descriptive -Gender factors
DCF	Descriptive -Class factors
DRG	Descriptive -Reasons Given for studying on the HE Course
DFE	Descriptive -Reasons for studying HE in FE Environment
DPC	Descriptive -Effects of pastoral care
DFT	Descriptive -Familiarity of tutors
DTP	Descriptive -Teaching practices that caused changes
DNK	Descriptive -Impact of new knowledge
DEO	Descriptive -Effect of New Knowledge upon Others
NER	None Expected Responses

Appendix Two

Table Two

The following table demonstrates the coding for participants

Code   **Participants (names anonymised)**

1TTJ	Teaching Team	Janet (Author)
2TTS	Teaching Team	Saul
3TTV	Teaching Team	Vincent
4TTJS	Teaching Team	Jess
5TTD	Teaching Team	Dana
6TTL	Teaching Team	Len
7TTC	Teaching Team	Carol

8Y1J	Year 1	Jack
9Y1L	Year 1	Lana
10Y1K	Year 1	Kitty
11Y1S	Year 1	Sonia
12Y1JS	Year 1	Jezebel
13Y2R	Year 2	Ruth
14Y2A	Year 2	Angela
15Y2W	Year 2	Winifred
16Y2J	Year 2	Jacinta
17Y2C	Year 2	Cathy
18Y3C	Year 3	Carlos
19Y3T	Year 3	Tina
20Y3M	Year 3	Mabel
21Y3S	Year 3	Sally
22Y3A	Year 3	Anita
23PSR	Previous Student	Roxy
24PSB	Previous Student	Benny
25PSS	Previous Student	Sam
26PSC	Previous Student	Candy
27PSJ	Previous Student	Joan

Appendix Three

The following table demonstrates the descriptive responses to Interview Question 1

: 'Tell me about your experience of education since leaving school please'

Participant status	Gender Factors DGF	Age Factor DAF	Previous T+L Q1 Positive	Previous T+L Q1Negative	Familiarity DFT	Pastoral Care DPC
1TTJ	F Yes	Yes epoch	Undergraduate	School	No	Negative School
2TTS	M N/A	Yes youth	English Lit Teacher	School	Yes	Negative School
3TTV	M N/A	N/A	Access	School	No	N/A
4TTJS	F Yes	Yes youth	Access	School	No	Negative School
5TTD	F Yes	Yes youth	Access	School	Yes	Yes Access
6TTL	M N/A	N/A	No	School	Negative	Negative School
7TTC	F Yes	Yes epoch	No	School	No	Negative School

8Y1J	M N/A	N/A	Access	NVQ	Access	Yes Access
9Y1L	F	Yes youth	None	School	None	Negative School
10Y1K	F	Yes family	Access	Nursing	Access Yes	Yes Access
11Y1S	F	Yes family	Access	School	Access Yes	Yes Access
12Y1JS	F	No	Access	O.U	Access Yes	Yes Access
13Y2R	F Mother	Yes older	Nursing	A Levels	N/A	N/A
14Y2A	F	Yes youth	Access	School	N/A	N/A
15Y2W	F Mother	Yes youth	Subjects	School	N/A	N/A
16Y2J	F	Yes youth	Access	School	Access Yes	Yes Access
17Y2C	F	Yes youth	School	A Levels	Yes/No	Yes/No
18Y3C	M	N/A	Access	School	N/A	N/A
19Y3T	F Mother	Yes family	College	School	N/A	Negative School
20Y3M	F Rebel	N/A	Access	School	Access Yes	Yes Access

300

21Y3S	F OCD	N/A	N/A	School	N/A	N/A
22Y3A	F	N/A	Community	School	N/A	N/A
23PSR	F Home	Yes wiser	N/A	School	Negative	Negative School
24PSB	M	Yes older	N/A	N/A	Yes- like teacher	Yes School
25PSS	M	N/A	Access	N/A	Access Yes	Yes Access
26PSC	F	Yes youth	Research	Group	N/A	N/A
27PSJ	J	Yes epoch	Access	School	Yes	N/A

Appendix Four

Table Four

Representative Examples of Descriptive Responses arising - Interview Question 2 'Tell me how teaching practices have impacted on your learning inside and outside of class – in a positive and negative way'.

Participant status	Impact Inside of class	Impact Outside of class	Positive Impact upon overall life	Negative Impact upon overall life
1TTJ	Excitement	Empowerment	Proud to be WC	Unsettled
2TTS	Encouragement	Self-analysis	Analysis/ ideas	None
3TTV	Question everything	More critical	Lateral thinking	No switch off
4TTJS	Opinion counts	Don't accept	Self esteem	Media/critical
5TTD	Able to speak views	Spread the word	Confidence	Marriage
6TTL	Thinking critically	Want to teach	Inspired	None
7TTC	Interest/ensnared	Compassionate	Empowerment	Critical (of everything)
8Y1J	Enjoyment	Teach family	Reduced anxiety	None
9Y1L	Hate capitalism	Question (More Cynical)	More radical	Argue more

11Y1S	Love Sociology	No answers/Cynical	Enthusiastic	None
13Y2R	Question More	More political	More critical	Cynical
14Y2A	Think outside box	Pressure on myself	Confidence to question	Cannot get it out of head
17Y2C	Courage to Question	More critical	Confidence	None
21Y3S	Learn from others	More empathy	Confidence to question	None
24PSB	Enjoyment	Helps others	Application of theories	Competitiveness
27PSJ	Enthusiasm	New ideas/ thoughts	Confidence to question	None

Appendix Five

Table Five

Responses given by all participants to key words (prompts)

Interview Question 4

'I have a list of words that describe the themes I think

are important regarding student learning experiences

which I would like to share and discuss with you.

But before we discuss these themes would you rank them

in order of what you think are the most important please?'

Key

P.S. = Participant Status

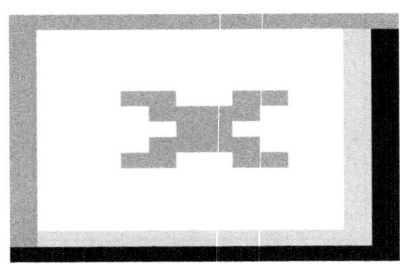

P.S	D.Q4D	O.Q4O	E.Q4E	F.Q4F	T.Q4T	E.Q 4EL
1TTJ	1	1	1	1	1	1
2TTS	5	6	3	4	2	1

3TTV	5	6	2	4	3	1
4TTJS	3	6	1	2	4	5
5TTD	6	5	2	4	3	1
6TTL	2	6	1	3	1	1
7TTC	2	3	3	1	2	2

8Y1J	5	6	4	3	2	1
9Y1L	N/A	3	N/A	N/A	2	1
10Y1K	6	5	4	1	3	2
11Y1S	4	6	2	1	3	5
12Y1JS	1	6	3	2	5	4

13Y2R	2	N/A	1	2	1	1
14Y2A	3	6	2	1	4	3
15Y2W	3	2	3	3	3	1
16Y2J	5	6	4	3	2	1
17Y2C	4	4	1	2	3	3

18Y3C	3	6	1	1	2	2
19Y3T	5	6	4	3	2	1
20Y3M	6	4	5	3	1	1
21Y3S	6	5	1	2	4	3
22Y3A	5	6	1	2	3	4

23PSR	6	5	1	3	2	4
24PSB	5	6	3	4	2	1
25PSS	3	6	2	1	5	4
26PSC	4	6	1	2	5	3
27PSJ	1	1	1	1	1	1

Table Six

Summary and Overview of all responses given to the key words

(prompts) used in Interview Question 4

R.N = Rank Number

D. Q4D = Democracy

O. Q40 = Oppression

E. Q4E = Equality

F. Q4F = Freedom

T. Q4T = Transformation

E. Q4EL = Enlightenment

R.N	D.Q4D	O.Q4O	E.Q4E	F.Q4F	T.Q4T	E. Q4EL
1	3	2	11	8	5	14
2	3	2	5	7	9	3
3	5	2	5	7	7	4
4	3	2	4	4	3	4
5	7	4	1	0	3	2
6	5	15	0	0	0	0
N/A	1	0	1	1	0	0

Appendix Seven

My transcript produced from the interview questions

1. Tell me about your experience of education since leaving school please?

At school I felt that I was a round peg in a square hole. I gained a scholarship to go to a very posh Grammar school, but I was working class and my family was not very well off. All the other girls at the school, an all girls' school, were very well off and came from very wealthy backgrounds and it made me feel different. They stayed on and did their A levels and things, but I left as soon as I could because at that time I'd already met my husband to be and so I just went and got the first job I could. I had my children when I was very young and then I kept taking every part time job I could because I was the bread-winner and my husband stayed at home to look after the children, but every time I applied for a job I had to put on the application form my qualifications, which were in poetry reading rather than anything academic. After a major falling out at my last job, I walked out and went straight to College and took courses in O levels and A Levels and then started an O U Degree. I then decided I wanted to do a Degree with other people rather than the solitary experience of doing an O U Degree, so I started another Degree in a University and then went on and did my Masters in Science and a Masters in Education. This enabled me to get my first teaching job so I went on and did my teaching qualifications.

2. Tell me how teaching practices have impacted on your learning inside and outside of class – in a positive and negative way.

I think my teaching practices have impacted upon me in a very positive way, in that I am able to recognise the struggles of my working class students - who are virtually all working class, - both financially and in terms of their confidence levels. I think this makes me a more empathic teacher in that I believe once I can instil the confidence to do well in my students I have broken down a major barrier for them. I also feel that my teaching practice has gained me a far reaching experience of different people's opportunities and barriers in education and because I teach Sociology, this is mainly about the concepts of class, gender and race. I also feel that after teaching a lot of Marxism Sociology I can see how the structures in Society have such a huge impact on people, far more than they realise, until they study sociology. It is hard to think of any negative things, except that when I have lost students through illness, or death I have felt considerable pain, but apart from that I cannot think of any other negative experiences, or affects.

3. What are the key themes/ideas that have emerged for you from these learning experiences?

I suppose the key things from my working class background and my education and teaching practices is that you have to fight to bring about the changes you want. When I was in my teens I was always very rebellious and joined several protest groups, such as CND Animal rights protests, fights against racism and that sort of thing and inside of me although I was a bit pessimistic about bringing change, I now know as I did then that we don't have to accept everything, we can bring about change. I suppose for me this was demonstrated with the Poll Tax. It just showed that there is such a thing as people power and if enough people fight against injustice, we can do something about it. So I think that is the main thing that has changed for me since I became a teacher, in that I cannot only bring about changes in Society as an individual, I can raise awareness about the inequalities in life with my students, in the hope that they will also bring about changes themselves.

4. I have a list of words that describe the themes I think are important regarding student learning experiences which I would

like to share and discuss with you. But before we discuss these themes would you rank them in order of what you think are the most important please?

When I first gave the participants these words to look at, I really did not realise how difficult it is to give them a particular score, mainly because they are all so important and dear to me as an individual. So I think I am going to follow the pattern of one of the participants and score them all as a 1.

5. Can you clarify as to why you chose some of the themes as being more important than others?

__Democracy,__ is a wonderful idea and one that I hope one day everyone in society will recognise and accept, unfortunately, in order to be totally democratic, the rich and powerful people would have to make sacrifices and I am not sure that is every possible, so it is a wonderful idea, but in reality I am somewhat pessimistic that it will every happen, - true democracy.

__Oppression,__ even as a child I can remember proudly walking around with a suitcase, even though it had nothing in it, with the words I *had written on it 'No colour bar in England'. To me that was oppression, that was what it was all about, the colour of someone's skin, denoting whether they were oppressed, or not. As an adult, I now realise that oppression can be something that is not only about physical elements, but more importantly perhaps it is about the oppression of mind as well. Since I started this EdD, Freire's work where he talks about oppression in Education is now for me a true and living example of how people can be oppressed in terms of their thinking. To add to that, as an A Level student, we had to read 1984 and that as well truly opened my mind as to how debilitating oppression of the mind is. So for me, education has changed my feelings about oppression, from not only being about physical oppression, but more about the oppression of thinking.*

__Equality,__ again is a wonderful concept, but the over-riding question for me is as one of my fellow teacher's said, who do I want to be equal with? I suppose the answer to that, is, surprisingly perhaps - I am happy with the identity I have. Yes, it would be lovely to be equal with somebody rich and not have to worry about my mortgage and other bills, but would I be willing to walk on others to gain that

313

wealth - and for me the answer is no. So I will strive in society to make people aware of the inequalities in life for others, particularly in education, but for myself equality is more about being in tune with your own self and I am happy with that.

Freedom, I suppose because I lived as a hippie for many years and I still have the principles of wanting peace and I worry about war and things, because of that when I think of freedom I cannot help but think of Bob Dylan's words when he said 'are the birds really free of the air', so I suppose realistically no one can ever have total freedom from our physical and psychological needs until the point of death, which I suppose is behind the saying 'rest in peace'.

Transformation, Yes I have definitely been transformed by education, as well as my life experiences in that I am not so naive as when I was a child, although I am still very much in touch with my child within. What started me wanting to do my doctorate was seeing how students said they had been transformed by doing the Degree and I have seen it myself. This is also coming out in their interviews with me and their personal statements, they make at the

314

end of the course. I am not sure that this transformation has brought about total happiness for them, but at least now they are more aware of the inequalities in society and I think this has engendered a feeling of non-acceptance for them as individuals. I also think that their transformation and my own has brought about a feeling of there being so many unanswered questions in life, I accept this and I am happy with this, but I am not too sure that my students find this an acceptable situation for themselves.

Enlightenment, *well every time I find out something new I get a real buzz from it and I suppose my main enlightenment through life has been due to education. When I am in a room with people discussing things that I previously did not understand and was too ashamed to let this be known, when I did finally understand, it was like a weight had been lifted off my shoulders. I did feel enlightened in every sense of the word as soon as people talked about things in a way I could understand them rather than the words written in a text book in somewhat dry academic terms. So for me enlightenment has been mainly about education, although perhaps one of my life experiences, that of becoming a mother gave me a huge feeling of* *enlightenment with regards to my own mother's struggles and feelings. So for me, enlightenment is about life experience and definitely about education.*

6TP. Finally, can you tell me how the experiences of being a student in these classes have affected your teaching practice?

Doing the O U Degree, as a student was great in that I had all the resources necessary laid out for me and I could access a tutor occasionally, but it was such a lonely and confusing experience. I found it really distressing, not to be able to ask someone even about the most simple things because I felt too ashamed to say that I didn't understand something, for example the first time I tried to listen to an audio tape from the O U the words kept telling me to refer to the course reader and I couldn't understand why I had not been given this book to read and so I panicked. I was then in floods of tears and kept saying to myself why haven't I got a course reader, which I clearly need to do this assignment. My husband then said maybe they mean books that are associated with the course content, rather than a particular book called that. From that moment on I felt a

huge sense of relief because of course he was right, but I also felt
that because I hadn't been able to understand the academic
terminology on the tape I must be a bit 'thick'. I now realise this is
how my students might feel if they haven't got any one to talk to. So
my teaching practice always involves class discussions and giving
the students the confidence to be able to ask anything they want
without feeling 'thick'. So, for me my life experiences and my
academic journey are definitely reflected in my teaching practices.

Printed in Great Britain
by Amazon

86509068R00181